GENDER AND CONFLICT TRANSFORMATION: Nagaland and Egypt

GENDER AND CONFLICT TRANSFORMATION: Nagaland and Egypt

Triveni Goswami

AKANSHA PUBLISHING HOUSE
NEW DELHI-110002 (INDIA)

AKANSHA PUBLISHING HOUSE
4649-B/21, Ansari Road
Darya Ganj, New Delhi - 110 002
Ph.: 23263193/9811582579
Fax: 011-23263193
Email: ektabooks@yahoo.com

Gender and Conflict Transformation: Nagaland and Egypt

First Published 2007

ISBN-978-81-8370-119-8

PRINTED IN INDIA

Published by Akansha Publishing House, New Delhi and Printed at Aryan Enterprises, Delhi.

CONTENTS

LIST OF MAPS

FOREWORD

Human issues and problems have commonalities despite the varied territorial and societal settings in which they occur. When the problems surface out of armed conflict, human sufferings of diverse nature and dimension engulf a sizeable section of the people living in the conflict area. Women and children, as the weakest component of the society, become the most visible and vulnerable targets of violence and exploitation of all forms of grave magnitude. When violence becomes the order of the day, the law is written by the perpetrators who tend to demolish the existing social order. The rights of women then become the first casualty. Thus, the history of conflict in different parts of the world is the history of suffering and injustice done to women. The root cause of one conflict could be different from the other, but the nature of women's suffering is similar in all cases. It raises the issue of gender in a conflict situation as a focal point for serious discussion for academics, policy makers and social interventionists.

It is a daunting but fascinating task to make a comparative study of gender issues in two situations where the societal framework is as different as the geographical contours. Yet there are striking similarities. The issues of human rights violations, social injustice and deprivation, the boundaries and limitations imposed on women by patriarchy are more or less similar. The forces and processes of social transformation are also more or less identical. Similarities could be found in the approach to mitigate the gender related problems. A comparative study of gender and conflict transformation in two different settings is indeed a rewarding exercise in understanding the issues in various contents and forms.

Triveni Goswami's seminal research covering gender and conflict transformation comparing two different geographical and socio-cultural settings is a pioneering work that deserves the attention of the academic world. A UNESCO fellow placed in Bibliotheca Alexandrina, the scholar has made a commendable attempt to figure out the gender related issues in two prominently different settings where one finds no meeting point. Despite diversities of grave import, both the Egyptian and the Naga societies have commonalities. Both are homogeneous on religious counts. Egypt is essentially a Muslim state with 90% of its population belonging to the Islamic faith. Nagaland represents similar homogeneous character with its overwhelming Christian population (90%). Both have been reeling under the scepter of violence for several decades although the roots of violence are of different natures. While Nagaland has been experiencing a massive and violent secessionist movement since Independence, Egypt has been suffering under a long spell of armed conflict spearheaded by Islamic militants. Both the societies are undergoing social transformation in which women as an independent variable have been playing a crucial role. In an era of information revolution, when people are exposed to developmental dynamics of wide varieties, the latent urge for social transformation in the framework of empowerment and gender equality cannot be stifled by the outdated patriarchy. The signs of societal development in a positive sense, even in the midst of perilous problems of violence, cannot be obliterated by the tantrums of obdurate forces of revivalism. Dynamic forces overpower recuperating static syndromes. The feminist platforms in Egypt and Nagaland, with their pro-active agendas signal the awaiting social transformations.

Triveni's book has grown out of her engagement in an empirical research in Nagaland and her thorough studies at Bibliotheca Alexandrina Institute of Peace Studies as a UNESCO Fellow. Her task has been challenging. The two settings are different making it difficult to undertake a comparative approach to understand and analyze the gender issues in Egypt and Nagaland. Both the societies are confronting the winds of change and social transformation, which might eventually lead to a sustainable conflict transformation. Nonetheless, it is fascinating to see how a young scholar has acquired mastery over an arduous task with an intellectual flavour and style. Triveni represents that generation of young scholars on whom rests the future of intellectual discourses. Her work is a repository of a wealth of empirical and historical information and analyses which form the spear point for positive and creative thinking on gender related issues in countries which are experiencing the surging currents of modernization, and social and conflict transformation.

Abu Nasar Saied Ahmed
Professor, Omeo Kumar Das Institute of Social Change and Development, Guwahati

PREFACE

The nature of conflict has undergone tremendous transformation over the last decade. Conflicts are no longer confined to a particular area or region. The forces of globalization have ensured that they have a spill over effect across territorial boundaries, triggering off changes within the socio-political and economic scenario. Contemporary conflicts are fast adopting alternative methods of warfare, penetrating into towns, villages and homes of the common people. In many parts of the world, the use of systematic force through insurgency, reduction of democratic space, violations of human rights etc. have resulted in perpetuating fear and insecurity and thereby, fragmenting the emotional fabric of the community.

In various sites of conflicts, it has been witnessed that the women are utilized as agents of protest and once the objective of the struggle is achieved, they are relegated to the background. The mobilization of women for the purpose of furthering the cause of a struggle and then pushing them to the vestiges of public memory is fast emerging as a popular truth in many cultures today. Often considered as the moral guardians of their community, women are vulnerable targets and are therefore subjected to various forms of violence, both physical and psychological. In a tussle for power between competing forces, the woman's body often emerges as the medium through which the nationalist discourse is spoken.

Within the context of overwhelming structural violence endemic in a society, women have emerged as agents of change. Utilizing their hitherto untapped potential as reservoirs of strength, women have initiated efforts of reconstructing their fragile, conflict-torn communities. Their peacebuilding efforts incorporate both social reconstructions of the community as well as the creation of a socially integrated and just order cutting across divisive ethnic lines. Adopting context specific strategies, they make efforts to involve all sections of the society. Their movement is operational on different fronts, incorporating issues of territorial security and social order while nurturing the capacity building potential of the community.

This book is the culmination of a 6-month *UNESCO/ Suzanne-Mubarak/Japan-Egypt Friendship Research Fellowship for the Empowerment of Women in Peace and Gender Studies (2006 Cycle).* As part of the Fellowship, I was based in Alexandria, Egypt, for a few months and in Nagaland for the rest. My study was a comparison of two seemingly contrasting contexts of Nagaland and Egypt. Although, they appear to be diametrically opposite social contexts, there were several common threads binding the two. Both of them are experiencing conflicts on similar lines between the State authorities and the Revivalists. The difference is in the nature of the Revivalist Movement. While in Egypt, revivalism has taken a religious hue, in Nagaland, the revivalist movement is coloured by shades of ethnicity. Nagaland, a largely tribal state in India's Northeastern region has given birth to India's longest guerilla movement, which is continuing till date. Egypt, on the other hand, has witnessed successive changes in the political regimes and has also been witness to a resurgent movement in religious conservatism over the years.

In both these contexts, women have had to bear the brunt of the repercussions—social, political, economic, religious and psychological. The respective prevalent nationalist discourses seeped in religious and ethnic fervours has shaped their self and identity. Much of who they are and what they have become, has to do with the manner in which their social identity, as guardians of the moral boundaries of their communities have been constructed. Each social scenario is beset with unique problems of its own and women, being the most vulnerable section, are caught in the never-ending vortex of complications.

Yet, despite these difficulties, women in both these contexts have emerged as agents of transformation. They have initiated efforts by bringing together like-minded people and organizing movements of change as both individuals as well as collectives. Taking up socially relevant issues plaguing their communities, they have taken a step forward in emancipating women from the clutches of socially depraving conditions and institutions. They have been instrumental in raising questions on previously taken-for-granted realities and have initiated a process of change in their respective communities. These are some of the issues that have been addressed in the book.

The journey to the ancient land of Egypt has truly been an enriching experience that would not have been possible but for the invaluable help that I received from several quarters. I would like to thank the Ministry of Human Resource Development, Government of India, for nominating my candidature for the prestigious Fellowship and to UNESCO for selecting me. I am particularly indebted to Dr. Mayssah Elnayal, Head of the Department of Psychology, University of Alexandria, who painstakingly took time out of her busy schedule to supervise my work at every step. I would also like to thank Dr. Azza Elkholy, the Co-ordinator of the Fellowship Programme in Bibliotheca Alexandrina, for facilitating my stay in Alexandria and to Ms. Fadoua Amer for being a trusted friend and a guide and for helping me in all possible ways in making my stay in Alexandria comfortable.

The staff and librarians at Bibliotheca Alexandrina were very helpful in granting me access to the materials in their custody. I am grateful to all of them. I would also like to thank Ms. Rachel Jakubowicz and Mr. Ali Zaid of UNESCO, Paris for answering all queries related to the Fellowship and for the smooth disbursal of the Grant. I appreciate the kindness and love of Catherine de Borchgrave, Programme Manager (NGOs, Human Rights and Civil Society), European Union, and Albert Carton who made me a part of their family. The Kikon family in Dimapur gave me invaluable support during my stay in Nagaland. I am extremely grateful to them. My special thanks are also due to Professor A.N.S. Ahmed, Professor Anuradha Dutta and Professor Partha Ghosh, for their constant encouragement and support. My fellow colleagues from the other countries helped me in a variety ways. Interacting with them was indeed a tremendous learning experience. I extend my appreciation to all the participants in my study without whose help and cooperation this work would not have been possible.

I would also like to thank Muhammad Imran Khan for taking time out of his otherwise busy schedule to design the cover for this book. Finally, I would like to extend my gratefulness to Akansha Publishing House, New Delhi, for publishing this book.

Triveni Goswami

INTRODUCTION

Gender issues cut across all sections of society, regardless of their political, economic and social contexts. The socially constructed view of gender is deeply imbued in popular imagination, which is intricately linked to age-old traditions. Because of less development, Third World societies suffer from the problem much more than the developed world. The roots of women's subordination are embedded, internalized and institutionalized within a societal framework. Against the background of unfinished nation building processes coupled with growing ethno-religious assertions, women in the third world societies are often used as cultural symbols to the detriment of gender equality. Whenever any form of upheaval occurs within a patriarchal framework, it has a spill over effect and more often than not, women become the first targets of victimization. In an effort to protect the society, the symbols of womanhood and their space are besieged. Restrictions are clamped on them even as their bodies are used as tools of suppression. Perpetuation of male dominance thus becomes endemic. In situations of societal conflicts, this dichotomy becomes more glaring.

Control is an integral part of patriarchy that promotes as well as sustains military values. It is thus masculinity that maintains militarism. The construction of gender stereotypes that reflects the expectations of the society as to how a man and woman should behave helps in re-enforcing this patriarchal control. Whatever be the nature of conflict, it is evident that women are the most marginalized and disempowered section of the society, and are hence, the worst sufferers. This is more evident in oriental societies, which are more deeply rooted in patriarchy.

I would like to make a comparative analysis between the situations of North East India and Egypt, where two very different kinds of conflicts exist. Caught between the protracted battles of the State and the Insurgents in the former and the State and the Conservatives in the latter, the woman emerges as an easy victim. The North Eastern region of India with its mosaic of entangled ethnic discontents has been home to several ethno-political upheavals for the past five decades. The conflicts in this region have mostly been Low Intensity Silent Conflicts eating into the societal framework, systematically forcing upon the freedom and space of all individuals. The intrusion into gendered spaces are felt more intimately by the women whose body becomes an easy pawn in the protracted battle between the competing forces.

The North Eastern region of India provides us with many examples of spontaneous women's initiatives to reduce the impact of conflict and to structure peace and development in the region. The peace initiatives of the Naga Mothers Association (NMA), for example, represent the notion of motherhood for the political mobilization of women. In Manipur, the *Meira Paibies* (Torch Bearers) have been immensely successful in spearheading large-scale protest movements. Initially set up to combat social evils like narcotics and alcohol, they were soon in the forefront of struggles against human rights violations by the security forces. These and similar examples, reveal that women in Northeast India have been playing a prominent role in peace building efforts.

I

NAGALAND: A BRIEF HISTORY

Nagaland is a narrow strip of mountainous territory in India, bounded by Assam in the west, Arunachal Pradesh in the north and Manipur in the south. It also shares its boundary with Myanmar in the east. It lies between latitudes 26 degree 6 minute and 27 degree 4 minute north of the equator and between longitudes 93 degree 20 minutes and 95 degree 15 minutes east. The capital of Nagaland is Kohima. The state of Nagaland comprises of 11 districts namely, Kohima, Dimapur, Longleng, Zunheboto, Mon, Phek, Wokha, Mokokchung, Tuensang, Peren and Kiphire. There are at least 36 tribes and sub-tribes in Nagaland, each having its own language belonging to the Tibeto-Burmese group of languages.

In 1879, the British came and conquered parts of Naga territory and called the area Naga Hills. When the Simon Commission visited Kohima in 1929, the Nagas pressed a demand for independence. Thereafter, according to the Indian Constitution Act of 1935, the Naga Hills was allowed to remain an "Excluded Area". On the 20 February 1947, the Nagas demanded an Interim Government for a period of 10 years, to be effective prior to the departure of the British. A day before the Indian Union gained independence from the British colonial rule, on 14 August 1947, the Naga Nationalist Council (NNC) under the leadership of A.Z.Phizo, declared Independence and cabled this information to the U.N.O. On December 30, 1949, NNC made an announcement for a Sovereign State of Nagaland. On May 16, 1951, the NNC arranged for a voluntary plebiscite to determine the unity of the Nagas. The results revealed that 99% were in favour of a sovereign state. On November 15, 1954, the Indian Armed Forces resorted to mass massacre in the "free Naga" territory. The Naga Constitution was approved on January 14, 1956 and the Naga Federal Government was inaugurated on March 22 of the same year (Lasuh & Nuh, 2, p.147).[1]

The NNC, by successfully mobilizing the people of Nagaland, enforced a complete boycott of the 1952 General Elections in India. In 1956, the NNC under the leadership of A.Z. Phizo proclaimed the establishment of a government with its own constitution and a Naga Army. In the War of Liberation between the Indian Army and the insurgents that followed subsequently, large numbers of Naga soldiers perished. In

Map-1
Location of Nagaland in India

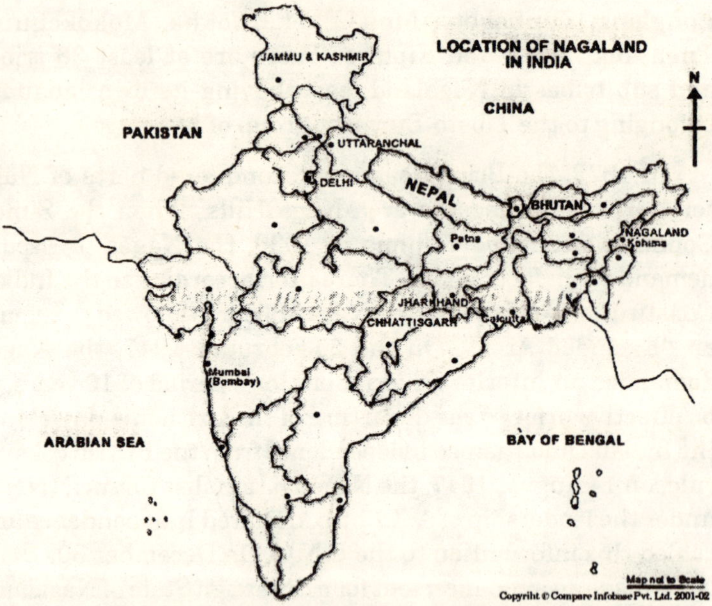

December 1963, Nagaland was conferred status of statehood within the Indian Union. Caught in the clashes between the Indian Government and the NNC, the common people suffered. This had serious fallouts, polarizing not only the Naga people but the NNC as well, into moderate and extremist factions. The moderate elements favoured a negotiated settlement. Taking this as an opportunity, in an effort to usher in lasting peace, the Naga Baptist Church took steps to facilitate the formation of a Peace Mission in 1964. The Peace Mission comprised of Jai Prakash Narayan, B.P. Chaliha, the then Chief Minister of Assam, and Reverend Michael Scott. The Mission's recommendations were rejected by NNC and thereafter the Mission was called off.

In 1972, the Government of India outlawed the NNC, Naga Federal Government (NFG) and the Naga Army. The Shillong

Accord between the Government of India and representatives of the underground organizations was signed in 1975, which resulted in the laying down of arms by a section of NNC. The Accord was repudiated by both A.Z. Phizo and Muivah. Soon, Muivah parted ways with the NNC and formed the National Socialist Council of Nagaland (NSCN). In 1988, there was a further split of the NSCN into the Isak- Muivah and Khaplang factions. The Konyak tribes formed the NSCN-K (Khaplang) under the leadership of Khole Konyak and S.S. Khaplang. Isak Swu and T. Muivah led the Tangkhul faction, the NSCN-IM. The rivalry between the two factions continues till date, creating fissures in the peace process in the region.

On February 23, 1996, Prime Minister of India, Narasimha Rao, offered to hold unconditional talks with the Naga insurgent groups. In June 1996, the United Front formed a Federal Government and Deve Gowda became Prime Minister of India. On November 5, 1996, NSCN (I-M) welcomed Prime Minister Deve Gowda's offer to open peace talks. Following a dispute within the coalition government, Inder Kumar Gujral succeeded Deve Gowda as the Prime Minister and on May 19, 1997, the United Front Government at the centre negotiated a ceasefire with the NSCN-IM camp, which later was also extended to the NSCN-K faction. The five-year-old process of negotiations with the NSCN-IM reached a high point in January 2003 when the leadership of the outfit collectively came to New Delhi for a round of talks. The ceasefire agreement with the Government of India has been renewed for the last couple of years. The latest development in the recent round of negotiations has been Muivah's agreement to scale down the demand for a sovereign Nagaland to a demand for *Nagalim*, an integration of the various Naga inhabited areas of India's North Eastern region.

Naga women for long have been associated with the peacemaking process. The grassroots initiatives for peace began with the ancient traditional institution of the *Pukhreila*

(Khashim, 1993, pp.193-194).[2]. Ever since then, women in Nagaland have actively participated in the efforts for peace both as individuals and as a collective force.

II

EGYPT: A BRIEF OVERVIEW

The Arab Republic of Egypt is located between 22 degree and 32 degree latitudes, north of the equator and between 24 degree and 37 degree longitudes, east of the Greenwich Median. Egypt lies to the North-Eastern part of the continent of Africa and is bordered by the Mediterranean Sea to its north; the Red Sea to its east; Palestine and Israel to its north-east; Libya to its west and Sudan to its south. A different form of conflict is seen in Egypt. Since Gamal Abdel Nasser became President, Egypt has witnessed a successive change of political heads with differing political affiliations, which have in turn shaped the dynamics between the State and the Islamic Conservatives. The reason I have used the term Conservatives instead of Fundamentalists is because the latter serves to homogenize and constrict our view of some Islamic thoughts and practices. The late 1980s and the 1990s witnessed resurgence in movements guided by the Islamic identity. Their efforts, incorporated among other activities, the use of the *Koran* as a tool for suppressing women and imposing restrictions on the cultural manifestations of womanhood, such as their dress and their mobility. The role of women in religious observances and education were also similarly restricted. In order to sustain the myth of masochism of man, the woman became the embodiment of suffering, whose very survival was dependent wholly on the support from the man.

Prior to undertaking this research project, my knowledge about Islamic Conservatives and the role of women's groups in Egypt were drawn from library research alone. There are several women's organizations such as Alliance for Arab Women, the Egyptian Centre for Women's Rights (ECWR),

Map-2
Political Map of Egypt

Egyptian Medical Women Association etc. that have been working for women's rights. These organizations have adopted several need-based approaches to ensure active participation of young women in decision-making and policy making processes. As an author has remarked, "*Women's movements in the Middle East are potential agents for democratization, yet they are highly constrained by the prevalent socio-political structures, lack of clear institutional targets and ambiguous state policies*" (Al-Ali, 2002).[3] In most countries in the Middle East, a shared understanding of Gender as a social category is intimately intertwined with the overwhelming reality of Islam.

The *Sharia* refers to the body of Islamic Law. The term means "way" or "path"; it is the legal framework within which public and some private aspects of life are regulated for those living in a legal system. It is based on Islamic principles of Jurisprudence. *Sharia* deals with many aspects of day-to-day life, including politics, economics, banking, business law, contract law, sexuality and social issues.

Two Muslim women considered leaders of the struggle for women's rights in Egypt are Huda Shar'awi and Zainab Al-Ghazali. Huda Shar'awi, founder of the Egyptian Feminist Union in 1923 is considered the Mother of the Egyptian Feminist Movement. A member of the upper class, she campaigned for women's voting rights, equal access to education and reform of Egyptian marriage laws. Zainab Al-Ghazali took a different view of Islam and the meaning of veil. She founded the Muslim Women's Association in 1936 and believed that Islam and not western style feminism, gave Muslim women the rights and freedoms they sought (http://mediaguidetoislam.sfsu.edu/03a_feminism.htm).[4]

My experience of working in the North Eastern region of India has revealed that although women are actively involved at the grassroots level, they are kept away from decision-making processes. This raises the issue of their access to power and the extent to which they are politically empowered. Hence, it needs to be examined whether women are relegated to being mere props in any movement of change or whether their voices are actually heard. An attempt has been made here to explore the possibilities of parallels, if any, in the situations in the North Eastern region and Egypt.

Review of Literature

The chapter *Theorizing Gender and Nation* in the book *Gender and Nation* by Nira Yuval-Davis speaks about how the notion of Manhood and Womanhood shapes the construction of our concept of the nation. The author states that although women are often regarded as the cultural symbols of the nation, they are excluded from the theoretical considerations of Nationhood and also denied their space from the public political sphere. In this chapter, the author has dealt with the various theories of gender relations, focusing mainly on three questions namely: First, why and how women are oppressed; secondly, the ontological basis of differences between men and women and thirdly, the differences among women and among men and their effects upon generalized notions of gender relations. According to her, the notion of the 'nation' has to be analyzed and related to nationalist ideologies and movements on the one hand and the institutions of the state on the other. Quoting various theorists, the author has also extensively dealt with the origin of the concept of the nation and the state.

The paper ***Women, Islam and the State: Subordination and Resistance*** by Tazeen Mahnaz Murshid deals with the emergence of the religious right wing in the political scenario of Bangladesh, and the impact it has had on the policies of the State as well as the women within Bangladesh. She traces the political history of Bangladesh and tries to show how successive regimes have dealt with gender policies. The author states how the *Purdah* reduces the mobility of the women and restricts the scope for full participation in national life. She then speaks about how the history of the resistance to subordination in Bangladesh has focused largely on three main issues, first, the manipulation of religion to ensure male domination; secondly, advocacy of economic emancipation for women and thirdly, revision of family laws. The author states that when the legitimacy of the State was linked with the Islamists, the latter's powers increased and with the taste of political power, the religious right (Jamaat –I-Islami) emerged as a contending force in the socio-political scenario of Bangladesh. In her conclusion, she stated that the state is unable to play an effective role as a mediator between these forces and the women who are often victims, because it effectively becomes a party to the perpetration of injustices against them.

The book *Women, Islamisms and the State: Contemporary Feminisms in Egypt* by Azza M. Karam deals with the impact of politicized Islamic discourse on women in Egypt. The author has analyzed the dynamics between the State, women and Islamists using Foucault's analysis of power. Thus, according to the author, the reactions and counter-reactions between these three forces are natural forms of power dynamics. The author has defined Feminists as those *women who are actively involved in articulating discourses on and of women, on a broad socio-political level*. She has spoken about three types of Feminist thoughts in contemporary Egypt. They are: Secular feminism, Muslim feminism and Islamist feminism. Both Islamist and Muslim feminists take recourse to the Qur'an in their efforts to champion women's rights. As the author states, *both sets of feminists argue against existing patriarchal religious formations/hierarchies, and the implications of their interpretations on gender.* While the Islamist feminists are more conservative in their approach, the Muslim feminists are more moderate in their outlook. For example, with regards to the veil, while the Islamist feminists believe that the veil is a signifier of religious obligation and conviction, the Muslim feminists consider the veil to be a matter of choice exercised upon by a woman. The third set of feminists spoken about by the author is the Secular feminist. According to the author, Secular feminists consider *religion a private matter for each individual but completely reject it as a basis from which to formulate any agenda on women's emancipation.* In her book, the author also speaks about the emergence of various women's organizations to work for the upliftment of women and strive for women's rights: socially, politically and economically. The author speaks about how the Egyptian State is interventionist, by formulating policies and laws that seek to control the popular, everyday discourse on gender. The author then goes on to speak about the dynamic relations between the State, the Islamic Revivalists and the Feminists. According to the author, the agenda of the prevalent political Islamist discourse is the Islamization of the people and the government. In achieving their stated purpose, they often find themselves at loggerheads with both the women's organizations as well as the state machinery. According to Foucault, resistance in itself is a form of power. Wherever there is power, there is a possibility of resistance. Islamists as well as the state are both regimes, although their sources of power are different. The women become sites of struggle and resistance in the interplay of power dynamics with the State as well as the Islamists. In conclusion, the author states that the need of the hour in Egypt is for a joint platform to fight for women's issues and their rights. A dialogue on common goals by the feminists is of utmost necessity for women in Egypt.

In the paper, *State versus Islam: Malay families, Women's Bodies, and the Body Politic in Malaysia* by Aihwa Ong, the author deals with the impact of Islamic Revivalism and State politics on Malay womanhood and kinship. She explains how the domestic unit of the family becomes an object of social policy through health, educational and welfare programs. In her paper, the author shows how the concepts of kinship, gender and reproduction have been transformed by State policies and Islamic Revivalism. With the emergence of the Islamic Revivalists, the control of female sexuality to reinforce and strengthen male authority, increased manifold. The state policy of family planning began to be looked upon as a threat to national survival. The masses felt that if contraception was widely adopted, Malays would lose their voting power vis-à-vis the other races. The change to a capitalist agenda ushered in various changes. According to the author, women began to seek work outside and a large number of women had the money and social freedom to experiment with a newly awakened sense of self. This induced a sense of fear in men of female competition. They felt that their experience and knowledge was being challenged. Tracing the history of Islamic resurgence in Malaysia, the author states that successive Islamic groups have had a significant impact upon the social construction of gender relations and morality in the society. In her paper she focuses on the ABIM (Angkatan Belia Islam Malaysia or Islam Youth Movement of Malaysia), which rose to national prominence during the 1970s. In trying to define a new *umma,* the AIBM and *dakwa* groups sought to borrow ideas from foreign Islamic cultures rejecting the Malay-Muslim culture. According to the author, women in the Malay society became the most potent symbols of Islamic Revivalism. The mini-telekung (a cloth that tightly frames the face and covers the head, hair and chest) and the hijab made inroads into the Malay culture. Although, the women were being portrayed as someone with the moral capacity to construct and preserve the imagined Malay community, the female body emerged as a space of contesting struggles in the troubled socio-political landscape of Malaysia.

The paper "*The Women's Movement in Egypt with Selected References to Turkey*" by Nadje S. Al-Ali, deals with the emergence and evolution of the women's movement in Egypt and Turkey. She begins her paper by citing a few references on the women's participation in the 1919 revolution and subsequent rise of feminist activism associated with the renowned feminist activist, Huda Sha'rawi and the Egyptian Feminist Union (EFU). According to the author, the early feminist movement can be associated with the rise of nationalism. In her paper, she has cited several scholars who have argued that the women's movement came of age during the period between 1945 and 1959. In 1948, Doria Shafik created the Bint El-Nil (Daughter of the Nile) association to work for the political emancipation of the women and also campaigned for the upliftment of women. The author also traces the growth of the feminist movement with the successive changes in the political regimes of Egypt. According to her, the Egyptian feminist activism receded under the rule of Gamal

Abdel Nasser (1952-1970) when the State became strict, monitored all political activity and banned autonomous organizations. Certain women friendly laws were passed by the State although the conservative Personal Status Laws were retained. During Anwar Sadat's regime, women underwent a mixed bag of experiences. The Personal Status Law was reformed in favour of women's rights, although women experienced high rates of unemployment and inequality in the workplace. Speaking about the present context, under Hosni Mubarak's regime, the author states that the women's movement has re-emerged. In 1985, the Personal Status Law was amended due to strong opposition from the Islamists who perceived it to be anti-Islamic. Confrontations between the Islamists and the women's activists increased, especially with matters related to the Sharia. The author states that many activists in the Egyptian women's movement view the preparations of the United Nations International Conference on Population and Development (ICPD) in Cairo, September 1994, as a turning point in their efforts to create a feminist platform. The Conference created space for the discussion on variously held taboo topics like abortion, violence and reproductive rights. Although the ICPD raised hopes on several issues pertaining to women's rights, attacks by the Islamists pressured the government to compromise on several matters thus frustrating the expectations raised. The author feels that there is no single issue that propels a woman's movement. There are different goals and priorities in the women's movement, which get translated into various projects and activities. In this paper, the author has critically evaluated the role of the State. She feels that in order to encourage the growth of the women's movement, the State has to play a more proactive role, be less restrictive in its policies and not bow down to the pressures of the Islamic Conservatives.

In the book *Autonomy Movements and Federal India* by Bhupinder Singh, Chapter 3 'The Naga Insurgency' deals with emergence of the insurgency in Nagaland. The author clearly outlines the progression of the movement and the form it currently takes in the political consciousness of the people in the region. The roots of this movement have been traced to the late 1940's with the birth of the Naga National Council (NNC), which was originally set up with an agenda for social welfare and later took on political hues. The Naga Baptist Church played a significant role in initiating a dialogue for peace by forming the Peace Mission in 1964. The Shillong Accord was signed in 1975 between the Government of India and the moderate faction of the NNC, which was later repudiated by both Phizo and Muivah. Muivah's faction formed the National Socialist Council of Nagaland (NSCN). Inter- tribal rivalry led to the further division of NSCN in 1988. According to the author, the desire for peace has acted as a powerful incentive for renunciation of violence. In 1997 as well as in 2001, concerted efforts on both sides led to the declaration of ceasefire. The author concludes on an optimistic note stating that there is a latent aspect of a possible Naga settlement.

In the paper "*Nationalism and Gender: The Construction of Identity*" by Nicole Negowetti, the author has dealt with the notion of how Gender and Nation are interlinked. According to the author, the notions of nationalism, gender and sexuality are socially constructed and they play a significant role in constructing and shaping one another. The author states that women are often signified as bearers of ethnic collectivity and transmitters of its culture. In the nation building process, the nation is often symbolized as a Mother, the entire burden of the cultural collectivity being placed on women. According to the author, power struggles by guardians of the nation are played out over the female body—both physically and metaphorically. In this paper, Negowetti cites the reference of Mayer (2000) who states that "in addition to biological reproduction, the nation is also reproduced culturally, socially and symbolically through its members." Negowetti goes on to state that the construction of the feminine identity is closely interlinked with the prevalent religious discourse in the society. Women are often represented as symbols of purity and traditions of the nation. According to Martin (2000), disciplining the woman's body through the application of state laws can be defined as violence if it violates the civil rights of female citizens. The common construction of the identity of men is as nation-builders and hence protectors, whereas, women are seen as biological producers and collective bearers of nationhood.

The hypotheses adopted for the present study is that caught amidst the emerging trends of Revivalism, women in both Nagaland and Egypt, have adopted strategies to initiate change and usher in transformation within their respective communities.

The objectives of this study are the following:

- To explore how Revivalism (Islamic Revivalism in the context of Egypt and Ethno-centric Revivalism in the context of Nagaland) as an emerging trend, has impacted upon women's space and mobility.
- To study the historical evolution of women's struggles in both Nagaland and Egypt.
- Explore the strategies of resistance adopted by women's organizations in both the contexts.
- To explore the extent to which women in Nagaland and in Egypt are empowered politically, socially and economically.
- To explore the linkages between the policy makers and grassroots organizations (through policies and formulation of laws) in Nagaland and in Egypt.

Methodology

In trying to achieve the above stated objectives, the author was *adopt a qualitative approach and collate adopted educated data from both primary as well as secondary sources*. It was felt that taking a few *Case Studies* of the various Women's Organizations in Egypt as well as some Islamic Conservatives could help shed light on the dynamics of the relations between the State, Women's Organizations and the 'Islamic Conservatives in Egypt. To this end, the author has conducted *interviews* with the concerned individuals of organizations, using a questionnaire focusing on basic issues like historical evolution of the women's movement in Egypt; power dynamics between the State, Women's Organizations and Islamic Conservatives; Strategies adopted by the women's organizations towards the culture of peace; the extent to which policies of the State and the Islamic Conservatives have had an impact on the space and mobility of the women and the extent to which women are empowered in the society.

The essential idea of the proposed research is to capture the experiences of women's organizations in two diametrically opposite contexts. The aims are to understand whether women victimizations are in equal measure in both situations. Are they passively tolerating whatever they have been subjected to? Are they making useful societal interventions not only to aim for gender justice but also to restore peace and harmony? These are some of the research questions that the present study would address. This essential contrast makes the comparison most challenging and can throw up several pertinent questions when completed.

REFERENCES

1 Lasuh, W. & Nuh, V.K. (2002). *The Naga Chronicle*. New Delhi: Regency.

2 Khashim, R. (1993). *Social Changes Among The Nagas* (Tangkhul). New Delhi: Cosmo Publications.

3 Al-Ali, N.S. (2002). *The Women's Movement in Egypt with Selected References to Turkey. Civil Society and Social*

Movements Programme, Paper Number 5. United Nations Research Institute For Social Development (UNRISD).

4 http://mediaguidetoislam.sfsu.edu/03a_feminism.htm Accessed on 03/10/06

I

GENDER, CONFLICT AND STATE: THE DYNAMICS WITHIN

Conflict: Nature and Types

Conflict arises due to the clash of incompatible goals. It may be defined as a struggle or contest between people with opposing needs, ideas, beliefs, values or goals. According to Edward Azar (1990), conflict "arises from mutually incompatible goals between two or more parties where an effective coordinating or mediating mechanism does not exist"(http://iadc.iwa.org/en/Unit1.htm).[1]

The Carnegie Commission on Preventing Deadly Conflict conducted a three-year study, the results of which reveal a vast number of factors that are instrumental in making societies prone to warfare. They are as follows:

1) Weak, corrupt or collapsed states.
2) Illegitimate or repressive regimes.
3) Acute discrimination against ethnic or other social groups.
4) Poorly managed religious, cultural or ethnic differences.
5) Politically active religious communities that promote hostile and divisive messages.
6) Political and economic legacies of colonialism or the Cold War.

7) Sudden economic and political shifts.

8) Widespread illiteracy, disease and disability.

9) Lack of resources such as water and arable land.

10) Large stores of weapons and ammunition.

11) Threatening regional relationships.

The report also states "When long-standing grievances are exploited by political demagogues, the scene is set for violence." (Carnegie Commission on Preventing Deadly Conflict, 1997).[2]

Noted Conflict theorist, Johan Galtung, proposed an influential model of conflict in the late 1960s. The model encompasses both symmetric and asymmetric conflicts. He suggested that conflict could be viewed as a triangle with contradiction (C), attitude (A) and Behaviour (B) at its vertices. According to him, contradiction refers to the underlying conflict situation, which include the actual or perceived 'incompatibility of goals' between the conflict parties. Attitudes include the parties' perceptions and misperceptions of each other and themselves and it includes the elements of emotion (feeling), cognition (belief) and conation (will). The third component, Behaviour includes cooperative as well as coercive gestures, which signify either reconciliation or antagonism. (Miall, Ramsbotham, and Woodhouse, 1999, p. 14)[3]

Types of Conflict

The nature of conflict varies according to the context of the situation as well as the actors engaged in it. Conflicts can be of ethnic, political, social, economic and psychological in nature.

The complexity of the phenomenon of conflict is visible in its various manifestations. There are various types of conflicts and varying levels in which they can be played out. There are Intra-personal conflicts (conflicts within an individual regarding various values and choices), Inter-personal conflicts (conflicts between individuals), Inter-group (conflicts between groups), Intra-group (conflicts within a group). The Power dynamics operating between the contesting parties in conflict, shape the nature of the conflict.

According to Sanam Naraghi Anderlini (2003), conflict can be of several types, namely:

1) Resource based conflicts: Economic power access/ control over resources.

2) Conflicts over governance and authority: political power, participation, control.

3) Ideological Conflicts: Rival ideologies and values.

4) Identity conflicts: Ethnic, religious, communal identity- rivalry over access to resources, territory, political/military power, social justice (Anderlini, 2003).[4]

The socio-political landscape of the world today is marked by several enduring, long-term conflicts between diverse ethnicities and identity groups. In multi-ethnic societies, this problem has become more forthcoming in recent years. As communities become more aware of their political rights and social history, their demands increase. When one group begins to dominate over the others, neglecting their needs of political, social and economic security, hostilities begin to emerge to the surface, bringing conflicting interests to the forefront.

Theoretical Perspectives of Ethnicity

Ethnic diversity is a feature of virtually all societies and more so today, due to the effects of industrialization and globalization, with the flow of communities from one society to another. Ethnicity *per se* is not problematic. It is the manifestations of ethnicity, the potential with which it can displace all other loyalties to emerge as the central basis of identity that requires immediate attention.

Identity theorists have proposed three main approaches to Ethnicity: the Primordialist approach, the Instrumentalist approach and Constructivist approach. The *Primordialist approach* takes ethnicity as a fixed characteristic of individuals and communities (Issacs 1975, Smith 1986, Kaplan 1993, Connor 1994). The Primordial theorists stress on the uniqueness and significance of ethnic identity and see conflict as a derivative of ethnic differences. Critics of this theory argue about its lack of explanation regarding the emergence of new or transformed identities as well as relatively peaceful relationships shared by inherently different ethnicities. The *Instrumentalist approach* sees ethnicity as a tool used by individuals, groups and elites to obtain an end. (Glazer and Moynihan 1975, Steinberg 1981, Brass 1985, Rothchild 1986b). According to the Instrumentalist theorists, ethnicity is taken as a label or a set of symbolic ties that is used by political entrepreneurs for a political end. Critics of this theory argue that ethnicity is embedded in the societal framework and therefore cannot be acted upon by individuals. The *Constructivist theory* views ethnicity as a product of social processes. It emphasizes the social origins and nature of ethnicity. According to these theorists, ethnicity is not an individual attribute but a social phenomenon. They believe that social interactions shape the conceptions of ethnicity. As John Chipman states "One of the great cruelties of ethnic conflict is that everyone is automatically labeled a combatant—by the identity they possess—even if they are not. Thus ethnic conflicts in their extreme can become total conflicts (1993, 240)."(Lake and Rothchild, 1996, pp. 6-8).[5]

Ethnic Conflict

Ethnic conflict is caused by the collective fears of insecurity (social, political and economic) of the future. Ethnic activists and political entrepreneurs, operating within groups, reinforce these kinds of fears thereby creating fractures in the society. The most significant fear of any ethnic group in conflict, is the fear of loss of identity—the very core of an individual's being. The fears of being assimilated into the dominant culture weigh heavily in the minds and hearts of the people. In such scenarios, *Chosen traumas* and *Past glories* are often successful in invoking feelings of suspicions and misgivings amongst members of an ethnic community, fuelling hatred towards one another.

According to Lake and Rothchild, the causes of conflict may differ for Inter and Intra group conflicts. For the former, information failures, problems of credible commitment, and incentives to use force preemptively—also known as the security dilemma, can lead to the conflict. Manipulation and blatant ethnic appeals of ethnic activists and political entrepreneurs can cause intra-group conflict (Lake and Rothchild, 1996, p.8).[6]

Ethnic Groups have certain common characteristics. Each ethnic group has a collective proper name, a myth of common ancestry, shared historical memories, one or more differentiating elements of common culture, association with a specific homeland, and a sense of solidarity with significant sectors of the population (Wolff, in Wolff & Schneckener, 2004, p .3).[7]

Ethnic Identity can be politicized and be given a political hue. Many of the ethnic conflicts revolve around the political rights of a people over a contested territory. The territory possesses certain inherent characteristics such that it often emerges as a symbol of individual and collective identity and has a significant value as a source of control and influence.

According to Stefan Wolff, the Nature and Addressees of Ethnic Claims can be of the following kind: (Wolff in Wolff & Schneckener, 2004, p. 4)[8]:

TABLE 1

Nature of Ethnic Claim	*Addressee of Ethnic Claim*
Self Determination	**Host Nation**
• Internal	Catalans in Spain Ethnic Germans in South Tyrol Corsicans in France
• External	Albanians in Kosovo Basques in Spain East Timorese Tamils of Sri Lanka Eritreans Palestinians
Linguistic, religious, and/or cultural rights	**Host-State**
	• Community groups in India and Pakistan. • German minorities in Central and Eastern Europe.
Access to resources/ equality of opportunity	**Host-State**
	• Community groups in South Africa. • German minorities in Central and Eastern Europe.
Material and/or political aid/support	**Kin-State**
	• Greeks and Turks in Cyprus.

Nature of Ethnic Claim	*Addressee of Ethnic Claim*
	• Germans in South Tyrol (Austria). • German minorities in Central and Eastern Europe (Germany).
	Kin-Nation
	• Albanians in Kosovo. • Germans in South Tyrol (Austrians and Germans) • Tamils in Sri Lanka • German minorities in Central and Eastern Europe (Austrians and Germans). • Other external actors. • Albanians in Kosovo. • East Timorese. • Palestinians.

Territorial Claims can be secessionist, irredentist and /or autonomist in their nature. The North Eastern region of India is a microcosm of diverse ethnicities. If one studies the socio-political landscape of this region, one finds that the different ethnic groups present have made secessionist, irredentist and autonomist territorial claims at different points of time in history. According to Stefan Wolff, *secessionism* can be defined as "a political movement of a specified population group that drives a process at the end of which it hopes to have succeeded in detaching itself and its territory from its host-state and to have established an independent state of its own". *Irredentism,* on the other hand can be defined as a "state-based, but not necessarily government-backed, movement that seeks to retrieve an external minority, together with the territory from its host state it inhabits across an existing border, i.e., to add territory as well as population to an existing state". *Territorial Autonomism*, on the other hand has been defined as "the desire of the resident population (or a part thereof) in a particular territory to gain a measure of self rule within this territory without seceding from its host-state (Wolff in Wolff & Schneckener, 2004, p.5).[9]

In India, the states of Nagaland as well as Assam have witnessed separatist groups in their states waging a struggle for secessionism from the Indian nation for several decades now. In Nagaland, the struggle for secessionism has been spearheaded by the National Socialist Council of Nagaland (NSCN), by both the Muivah and Khaplang factions, whereas, in Assam, the separatist movement has been spearheaded by the United Liberation Front of Asom (ULFA). Besides this movement for secessionism, Assam also has several movements led by the various ethnic groups for territorial autonomism and irredentism. The Dimasa, an ethnic group in Assam, is spearheading a movement for the establishment of an autonomous state for Dimasas, called "*Dimaraji*" within Assam. This movement, like many others in the North Eastern region of India, contains strains of both autonomism as well as irredentism. This is because the conceptualization of the proposed state of Dimaraji would include all the Dimasa inhabited regions in the North East of India, implying that it would not only include the external minority i.e. the Dimasas but also the territory which they inhabit in a host state, across the border.

According to Stefan Wolff, the nature and level of territorial claims can be of the following kind: (Wolff in Wolff & Schneckener, 2004, p.6).[10]

TABLE 2

Nature of Territorial Claim	*Level of Territorial Claim*
Irredentist/Secessionist	Inter-state, inter-group, and group-state • South Tyrol pre-1946
Irredentist/Non-Secessionist	**Inter-state** • Alsace 1919-40
Non-Irredentist/ Secessionist	Minority versus Host-state and Inter-group • Kosovo • East Timor • Tamils of Sri Lanka • Eritrea • Basques • Catalans • Palestinians
Non-irredentist/non-secessionist/autonomist	Minority vs. host-state and inter-group • Corsica • South Tyrol since 1946.

According to Stefan Wolff, conflict issues and examples of their manifestation can be of the following kind: (Wolff in Wolff & Schneckener, 2004, pp.10-11)[11]

TABLE 3

	Minority	*Host-nation*	*Host-state*	*Kin-State/ Kin-nation*	*Other external actors*
Minority	Political goals and means to realize them. Intra-community disputes among Tamils, Kosovo Albanians, Palestinians and Basques.	Territorial control, equal access to resources. Catalans, South Tyrolese, Germans, Palestinians in the occupied territories.	*Territorial control (autonomy/secessionism). South Tyrol, East Timor, Eritrea, Corsica, Palestinian territories. *Minority rights and their implementation: India, Pakistan. *Equality of opportunity: South Africa.	Political goals and means to realize them. Tamils of Sri Lanka, Greeks and Turks in Cyprus.	Political Goals and means to realize them. Kosovo Albanians, Palestinians.
Host-nation		Political goals and means to realize them. Serb Resistance Movement after 1997-98 vs. supporters of President Milosevic over Kosovo policy. Hawks and Doves in Israel.	Access to, and control over, resources. Italians in South Tyrol. Right wing Israelis.	Interference, perceived disadvantages because of support of external minority. Italians in South Tyrol	Interference by external actors. Reaction in Serbia to NATO air campaign. Reaction in Israel to calls for restraint from EU and US.

	Minority	*Host-nation*	*Host-state*	*Kin-State/ Kin-nation*	*Other external actors*
Host-state			Political goals and means to realize them. Different political parties in India and Pakistan. Different political parties in Israel.	Territorial control: Cyprus. Human and minority rights policy: South Tyrol	Sovereignty: Kosovo, Israel
Kin-State/ Kin-nation				Political goals and means to realize them. Different political parties in Greece and Turkey.	Interference by the kin-state in an ethnic conflict in the host state: Cyprus.
Other external actors					Conflicting interest structures: Kosovo, Israel.

Protracted Social Conflict

Some conflicts emerge out of long-term antagonistic relationships shared amongst members of different identity groups. Such a scenario is particularly seen in communities that are multi-ethnic and where one identity group is dominant over the others. Such situations give rise to Protracted Social Conflicts. According to Edward Azar (1990), "Protracted Social Conflicts are based in deep seated racial, ethnic, and religious tensions that combine with structural divisions within societies and political oppression to result in the victimization of one or more group" (http://iadc.iwa.org/en/Unit1.htm).[12]

According to Azar, "grievances resulting from need deprivation are usually expressed collectively. Failure to redress these grievances by the authority cultivates a niche for a protracted social conflict" (Miall, Ramsbotham & Woodhouse, 1999, pp.73-74).[13] He cites security needs, development needs, political access needs, and identity needs (cultural and religious expression) as the basis of such conflicts. Azar believes that Protracted Social Conflicts tend to be concentrated in developing countries which are typically characterized by a 'rapid population growth and limited resource base' and also have restricted 'political capacity' often linked to a colonial legacy of weak participatory institutions, a hierarchical tradition of imposed bureaucratic rule from metropolitan centres, and inherited instruments of political repression (*Ibid*).[14] Many a time, these Protracted Social Conflicts evolve into long drawn Low Intensity Conflicts, wreaking havoc on the social, psychological and economic resources of a community. The term *Low Intensity Conflicts* (LIC) has been variously defined. One such definition of LIC is "political or military confrontation between contending states or groups, below conventional war and above the routine peaceful competition among states. It frequently involves protracted struggles of competing principles and ideologies. LIC are often localized, generally in the Third World but contain certain regional and global security implications" (Internet reference cited in Goswami, 2006, p. 24).[15]

The State and its Role in Conflict Scenarios

Most people derive their primary identity from the State. Different theorists have provided varying definitions of the nature of the State. In his definition of the 'modern state', Stuart Hall (1984) includes the following features: "power is shared; rights to participate in government are legally or constitutionally defined; representation is wide, state power is fully secular and boundaries of national sovereignty are clearly defined"(Yuval-Davis, 1997,p. 12).[16] Engels (1977) expressed the Marxist view on the nature of the State as "a power, seemingly standing above the society, that would alleviate conflict and keep it within the bounds of order; and this power, arisen out of society but placing itself above it, and alienating itself more and more from it, is the state" (Yuval-Davis, 1997,p. 13).[17] The State has also been defined as "a body of institutions which are centrally organized around the intentionality of control with a given apparatus of enforcement (juridical and repressive) at its command and basis...Different forms of the state will involve different relationships between the control/coercion twin which is the residing characteristic of the state" (Anthias and Yuval-Davis, 1989 cited in Yuval-Davis, 1997, p.14).[18]

Most conflicts in the contemporary world revolve around the notion of Statehood as it has the ultimate legitimacy of sovereignty. Edward Azar saw the State as being a central factor in the emergence of Protracted Social Conflicts. According to Azar (1986), since in Protracted Social Conflicts 'highly centralized political structures are sources of conflict', a solution could be brought about by fostering decentralized political systems (Miall, Ramsbotham &Woodhouse, 1999, p. 85).[19]

The nature of the political regime in a nation is intricately linked with the propensity for conflict. According to Miall, Ramsbotham and Woodhouse, conflict within a state can emerge in the following circumstances:

First, conflict can become endemic, even in established liberal democratic states, when party politics becomes ascriptively based and one community perceives that state power has been permanently 'captured' by another, and is therefore driven to challenge the legitimacy of the state in order to change the situation, as in Canada, Belgium, Spain (Basques) or Northern Ireland (Lijphart, 1977; Gurr and Harff, 1994, chapter 5). This has also been a feature of a number of non-western countries, such as Sri Lanka (Horowitz, 1991).Second, conflict is likely in countries where authoritarian regimes successfully manipulate the state apparatus in order to cling to power and block political access to all those not part of their own narrow patronage network, eventually becoming little more than exploitative 'kleptocracies', as in Mobutu's Zaire. Here, politics has indeed become zero-sum and change can only be effected through a direct challenge to the incumbent regime. Third, the growing phenomena of 'failed' or 'collapsed' states (Helman and Ratner, 1992; Zartman, ed., 1995), which in the absence of adequate means for raising revenue or keeping order, succumb to endemic and chaotic violence (Miall, Ramsbotham and Woodhouse, 1999, pp. 86-87).[20]

The functions and the role of the State are far reaching. It plays a significant role in mediating conflicts. The strategies adopted and implemented by the State can go a long way in resolving or escalating the conflict. Repressive measures by the State often lead to the escalation of the conflict. Conflict resolution analysts believe that power-sharing strategies are more effective than coercive measures, in conciliating conflicts.

Gender

Gender refers to the social and cultural codes used to distinguish between what a particular society considers 'masculine' or 'feminine' qualities, characteristics, attributes or behaviours. Gender is a cultural construction and shapes the cognition and behaviour of each sex. Gender affects how people perceive themselves and others. Since gender roles are culturally determined, with the passage of time, the gender roles evolve. Being a product of social construction, the expectations of what it means to be a man and a woman are shaped by the prevalent discourses of patriarchy in the society.

The normative understanding of womanhood is moulded by the dominant social discourse of the public/private divide. Women are expected to belong to the private sphere while men are expected to belong to the public sphere. By relegating women into the private domain, their voices are often hidden from public memory and their mobility and spaces are restricted.

Although women are readily accepted as the cultural symbols of a society as well as the moral conscience of the nation, for long they have been denied their rightful place in the socio-political arena. Women are often taken as the symbol of nationhood yet they are excluded from the theorization of nationalism. Men have the prerogative to shape the discourse on what or who constitutes the nation and in all of this, the woman is denied a voice. According to Anthias and Yuval-Davis, "women's oppression is endemic and integral to social relations with regard to the distribution of power and material resources in the society"(1992, cited in Yuval-Davis, 1997, p.7).[21]

Women are often the worst victims in any conflict that takes place in the society. Since women are believed to be the bearers of their culture and nationhood, whenever there is an attempt to discipline and control the processes of the nation, women are the first to be targeted. In an effort to "protect" them from the contamination of the enemy, women's bodies are subjected to restraint and control. Their spaces are invaded into, mobility is curtailed and cultural manifestations such as their attire are clamped upon. According to Martin (2000), "the disciplining of the women's body through the application of state laws can be defined as violence, when it violates the civil rights of female citizens or threatens their health, in the interests of the nation" (cited in a reference from the Internet).[22]

Thus, the notions of gender, conflict and state are interlinked and shape the construction of one another. When gender identities intersect with ethnicity and other religious identities, the socio-political landscape becomes more complex. Interactions and social exchanges between them give rise to new divergences and become a fertile ground for diverse social movements.

REFERENCES

1 http://iadc.iwa.org/en/Unit1.htm Accessed on 12/10/06.

2 http://iadc.iwa.org/en/Unit1.htm Accessed on 12/10/06.

3 Miall, H, Ramsbotham, O and Woodhouse, T (1999). *Contemporary Conflict Resolution*. UK: Polity Press and USA: Blackwell Publishers.

4 Anderlini, S.N. (2003) Causes of Conflict: A Brief Overview (Power Point Presentation for UNIFEM). *Women Waging Peace*.

5 Lake, D A & Rothchild, D (1996). *Ethnic Fears and Global Engagement: The International Spread and Management of Conflict*. Institute on Global Conflict and Cooperation. University of California, Multi-Campus Research Unit.

6 *Ibid.*

7 Wolff, S (2004). Managing and Settling Ethnic Conflicts. In: Wolff, S & Schneckener, U. (Ed.) *Managing and Settling Ethnic Conflicts: Perspectives on Successes and Failures in Europe, Africa and Asia*. UK: C. Hurst & Co. Ltd. (pp.1-17).

8 *Ibid.*

9 *Ibid.*

10 *Ibid.*

11 *Ibid*

12 http://iadc.iwa.org/en/Unit1.htm Accessed on 12/10/06

13 Miall, H, Ramsbotham, O and Woodhouse, T (1999).

Contemporary Conflict Resolution. UK: Polity Press and USA: Blackwell Publishers.

14 *Ibid*.

15 www.globalsecurity.org/military/library/policy/army/fm/100-20/10020gl.htm in Goswami, T (2006). Role of Women as Peace Builders with Special Reference to Nagaland. India: Peace Studies, Omeo Kumar Das Institute of Social Change and Development (OKDISCD), Guwahati, Assam.

16 Yuval-Davis, N (1997). *Gender and Nation*. London, New Delhi, California: Sage Publications.

17 *Ibid*.

18 *Ibid*.

19 Miall, H, Ramsbotham, O and Woodhouse, T (1999). *Contemporary Conflict Resolution*. UK: Polity Press and USA: Blackwell Publishers.

20 Miall, H, Ramsbotham, O and Woodhouse, T (1999). *Contemporary Conflict Resolution*. UK: Polity Press and USA: Blackwell Publishers.

21 Yuval-Davis, N (1997). *Gender and Nation*. London, New Delhi, California: Sage Publications.

22 http://www.skynet.ie/~peacesoc/read/nationmasculinity.html 14/09/2006.

II

EMERGING REVIVALIST TRENDS AND THE BREWING SOCIAL IMBROGLIO

The contemporary world has been a witness to revivalist trends both ethnic as well as religious in nature. The term 'Revivalism' has been variously defined. Revivalism can denote "spirit or activities characteristic of religious revivals" or alternatively, "a desire or inclination to revive what belongs to an earlier time" (www.thefreedictionary.com/revivalism).[1] While the former definition signifies the process of Religious Revivalism, the latter definition implies the process of Ethnic Revivalism.

Religious Revivalism

According to McLoughlin, "revivalism is a part of the periodic process of re-examining and redefining the social and intellectual values of a society. The religious aspects of these re-examinations have been called 'great awakenings'' (cited McLoughlin, 1959).[2] Religious revivalists invoke and revitalize the practices and ideas of an earlier time. In Christianity, revivalism is a predominantly North American Protestant phenomenon. The Christian revivalists urge the disciples to accept forgiveness of personal sin through faith in Jesus Christ and commit themselves to spiritual self-discipline. They also encourage the followers to engage in religious exercises such as prayer, *Bible* reading and support for the Church. Akin to the emerging revivalist trends in Christianity, the Islamic world has also been witness to a wave of revivalist trends. Since, the current work is focused on the women in Egypt, Islamic Revivalism will be dealt with in a greater detail.

Islam and Islamic Revivalsim

Before embarking on the issue of Islamic Revivalism, one must be introduced to the notion of Islam. **Islam** is a monotheistic religion characterized by the acceptance of the doctrine of submission to God i.e. Allah and to Muhammad, as the Prophet of God. According to Mohammad Ali Syed (2004), the Qur'an (which is believed by Muslims to be the word of God) was revealed in stages during the twenty-two years of the prophethood (*risalat*) of the Prophet Muhammad (pbuh). During the same period, the Prophet (pbuh) made statements and gave his approval or disapproval on various religious, moral, social, cultural and legal issues. These statements are called *Hadiths* and were collected by various Hadith collectors. Both the Qur'an and the *Hadiths* made it absolutely clear the Qur'an was the supreme and ultimate authority and a guide for all Muslims in all matters (Syed, 2004, p.5).[3]

"The Muslims submit to Allah through *arkan al-din,* the five basic requirements or 'pillars':

Shahadah – The affirmation that 'there is no god but God, and Muhammad is the messenger of God.'

Salah – The five daily ritual prayers.

Zakat – The giving of alms, also known as religious tax

Sawm – Dawn-to-sunset fast during the lunar month of Ramadan.

Hajj – The pilgrimage to Mecca"

(http://columbia.thefreedictionary.com/Islam+(concept).[4]

Islamic Revivalism entails a resurgent movement of revivalism generally characterized by moral conservatism and the literal interpretation of the Qur'an. There is also an attempt to implement Islamic values in all aspects of daily life. According to Esposito and Voll,

> In the Muslim world, there has been an important and highly visible resurgence of Islam. The affirmation of faith and identity is a powerful force in all aspects of human life and is reflected in clothing, changing social lifestyles, and the arts, as well as the more visible arena of politics and political power. Concurrent with this resurgence is a growing demand for greater popular participation in the political system (Esposito & Voll, 1996, pp.15-16).[5]

Islamic Revivalism in Egypt

Successive political regimes in Egypt have shared different relationships with the movement for Islamic revivalism in the society. The Muslim Brotherhood, a front runner of Islamic Revivalism, was established by Hasan al-Banna in Egypt in 1928. In the 1970s, the notion of Political Islam began to gain ground. Instead of merely being a reactionary force, groups such as the Muslim Brotherhood began to actively participate in the political arena to initiate political change and development. According to Esposito and Voll,

> much of the character and politics of contemporary Egypt has been influenced by the revolution of 1952 and the subsequent emergence and rule from 1952 to 1971 of Gamal Abdel Nasser. Nasser redefined the nature of Egyptian nationalism and promoted Arab nationalism and socialism both at home and abroad. He centralized and refined the apparatus of the authoritarian, 'security' state and projected himself as a regional and world leader (Esposito &Voll, 1996, pp.173-174).[6]

The rigid stance taken by Nasser towards Muslim Brotherhood brought forth the wrath and hostility of the latter. In 1966, Nasser ordered the execution of Sayyid Qutb, the chief ideologue of Muslim Brotherhood, and initiated a mass crackdown on the activists of the Brotherhood. Anwar Sadat succeeded Nasser as the President in 1971. Sadat was more flexible in his policies towards the Muslim Brotherhood and it was during his tenure that the jailed leaders of the Brotherhood were released. His policies towards the movement of Islamic Revivalism helped him gain legitimacy in the eyes of the people and also expand his popular support. Such a scenario gave birth to several other radical Islamic groups. According to Esposito and Voll, "among the major groups were the Islamic Liberation Organization (also known as Muhammad's Youth or Shabab Muhammad), Jamaat al-Muslimin (the Society of Muslims) or, as it was more popularly known, Tafir wal-Hijra (Excommunication and Emigration), Jamaat al-Jihad (Society of Holy War), and Salvation from Hell" (Esposito and Voll, 1996, p.175).[7] In the wake of increased radicalism, Sadat tried to rein in the forces of political Islam. Like Nasser, he clamped down on the revivalists and young students and professionals who were actively involved in the movement. His aggressive actions against the movement cost him his life and in 1981, Sadat was assassinated.

Hosni Mubarak succeeded Sadat as the President of Egypt. During the 1980s, political Islam as a movement got institutionalized. The society in Egypt witnessed a revival of Islamic consciousness and began acknowledging Islamic beliefs and values in their day-to-day life. The implementation of the Islamic ways of life became more visible in the social fabric of the community in Egypt. During the 1980s wearing new forms of Islamic dress, a phenomenon that had begun in the 1970s, now became more widespread and prominent among women in urban areas, especially among students and professionals in the middle and upper-middle classes. While some women took up forms of dress that completely covered their face and bodies and withdrew from public life, most preferred modern forms of Islamic dress, which they believed enabled them to function more freely in their professional lives and in urban areas that were overcrowded and in which the close proximity and contact between the sexes in public transportation and the workplace was frowned upon (Esposito and Voll, 1996, pp.177-178).[8]

The influence of the Islamic groups in Egypt still remains alive. Although the confrontations with the State have not been very visible in recent times, their presence in the social consciousness of the people as well as the socio-political landscape of the society is discernable.

Ethnic Conflict and Ethnic Revivalism

Ethnic Conflicts are a form of group conflicts in which the goals are expressed in terms of ethnic fractures in the community. Wolff has spoken about three types of ethnic minorities:

> (1) External minorities, i.e., minorities that, while living on the territory of one state (host state) are the ethnic kin of the titular nation of another, often neighbouring, state (kin-state), (2) transnational minorities, i.e., ethnic groups whose homeland stretches across several different states without their forming the titular nation in any one of them; and, (3) indigenous minorities, i.e., ethnic groups living in any ancestral homeland which is on the territory of just one state of which they are not the titular nation (Wolff in Wolff and Schneckener, 2004,p.2).[9]

According to Wolff, the Germans in South Tyrol, the Greek and Turks in Cyprus and the Albanians in Kosovo are examples of External minorities. The Tamils of Sri Lanka and India and the Basques and Catalans of Spain and France are examples of transnational minorities. Whereas, various identity groups in India, Pakistan, parts of South Africa, the Corsicans of France etc., are examples of Indigenous minorities (Wolff in Wolff and Schneckener, 2004, p.3).[10]

Ethnic Revivalsim

Ethnic Revivalism refers to resurgence in ethnic affiliations.

Ethnicity is not fixed but is socially defined. Ethnic Revivalists strive to promote, preserve and transmit their culture and ethnic identity, especially when they experience a threat of loss of their identity. According to George Bernstein (1984),

> Revivalist groups tend to use cultural symbols to express grievances, reinvesting cultural potency to empty symbols, or restoring social status to a displaced native culture. Such restoration becomes a way of expressing discontent, although the true sources may be economic, political or psychological insecurity. Often such groups find charismatic leaders who stimulate group anger and solidarity by lamenting the loss of cultural strength or the social status of the native culture (www.jstor.org/view/00405841/ap050108/05a00050/0).[11]

The wave of contemporary ethnic conflicts can be said to be influenced by several factors. First, the trend towards 'democratization' in previously authoritarian countries has provided opportunities for ethnic minorities to assert their group rights—perceived as well as real, more openly. Secondly, there is an ever-increasing concern among the international community for the rights of the ethnic minorities and thirdly, there is a legal gap left for the voluntary interpretation of the content and holders of self-determination rights (Gahramanova, 2006,p.153).[12]

Today, ethno-national sentiments are on the rise and in several parts of the world, a particular type of regime called "Ethnocracy" is fast emerging. According to Ivekovic and Mostov, ethnocracies are a type of rule that concentrates power in the hands of the leaders, who are successful in promoting themselves as uniquely qualified to define and defend the (ethno) national interests, and in which the ruled are collective bodies defined by common culture, history, religion and myths (http://www.skynet.ie/~peacesoc/read nationmasculinity. html).[13] According to Nicole Negowetti, "Ethnocrats argue that returning to 'our traditional values' will create order and stability out of the chaos of political disintegration and social turmoil. Community and religious practices tied to ethno-national customs provide one mechanism or supervision of women's bodies (Ibid).[14]

The ethnic schisms in the Balkans are very evident today and in fact; *Ethnic Balkanization* has become a reality in many parts of the world today and is making its presence felt in the North-Eastern region of India as well. The growing ethnic tensions in the region can be attributed to both geographical as well historical factors. First, geographical factors explain how the low mobility of the population leads to perseverance of ethnic identity and native languages as a point of reference for the right to self-determination. Secondly, contradictory interpretations of history i.e. "divergent national narratives"(a term used by Tom de Waal), helps in explaining how it can mobilize people to demand for greater rights for their group identity (Gahramanova, 2006, p.155).[15]

Political entrepreneurs take advantage of the emotionally charged members of an ethnic community and invoke *past glories* and *chosen traumas* as a mobilizational tactic. Playing upon the emotional sentiments of the people, they create discourses of violence. They are instrumental in constructing and perpetuating the discourse of hatred of the *other* and rigidifying the divide between *Us* and *Them*. According to Gahramanova, the "education system along with family socialization, are also potent sites for the discursive formation of ethnic identity along with political symbolism" (Gahramanova, 2006, p.167).[16] Apart from this, the mass media too plays a significant role as a breeding site of stereotype formation.

Self, Identity and Social Conflict

Self

As a psychological construct, Self is hard to define. William

James, the philosopher, theologian and psychologist, termed self "the most puzzling puzzle with which psychology has to deal" (http://www.psych.neu.edu/ISSI/daily.htm).[17] Some notions about the Self are as follows:

a) The self is reflexive—it can become the object of its own attention (from various perspectives)—and this reflexiveness underlies many of the activities of the self.

b) Most of our understanding of the world is filtered through our understanding of self.

c) Although the self is a stable entity, it manifests its fluidity as its different aspects surface to the fore, in varying situations.

d) Due to a variety of reasons—personal and interpersonal motives, the self on public display does not often match the self of which we are privately aware.

In a nutshell, the human self can be described as "a self-organizing, interactive system of thoughts, feelings, and motives that characterizes an individual. It gives rise to an enduring experience of physical and psychological existence—a phenomenological sense of constancy and predictability. The Self is reflexive and dynamic in nature: responsive yet stable"(Ibid).[18] No one knows the exact location of the self in the human body as well as its emergence in the human consciousness, as yet.

Sigmund Freud propounded the Psychoanalytic approach in psychology. His theory of personality focused on the instincts and sexual drives and he believed that across one's lifetime, different driving forces develop and shape our interactions with the world. The three components of the Id, Ego and Superego comprised of *Freud's structural theory of the self.* According to Freud, individuals are born with the Id. The Id is based on the Pleasure principle and is not very reality oriented. As the infant grows up, across the next three years of life, the interaction with the outside world increases and the second part of the personality begins to take shape. This part, called the Ego is based on the Reality principle and is the mature part of the personality. Its aim is to meet the needs of the Id as well as be in touch with the reality. By the time the child is of 5 years or by the end of the phallic stage, the Superego develops. The Superego is akin to the conscience, the moral safeguard, dictating our beliefs of right and wrong. According to Freud, the ego is the strongest –satisfying the whims and fancies of the Id, taking into consideration the reality as well as pampering to the needs of the Superego (http://allpsych.com/psychology101/defenses.html).[19]

Erik Erikson accepted Freud's view of infantile sexuality but believed that an individual's personality develops beyond five years of age. In fact, Erikson's theoretical approach encompasses the entire lifetime of an individual. Some significant characteristics of his theory are: -

a) The Ego is of utmost importance.

b) Part of the Ego is able to operate indcpendently of the Id and the Superego.

c) The Ego is a powerful agent that can adapt to situations thereby promoting mental health.

d) Social and sexual factors both play a role in personality development.

Erikson's theory was more comprehensive than Freud's, gave a more positive attribute to the Ego and emphasized on the interplay between the individual and the social processes in the development of the self. Erikson formulated eight stages in the development of the self. Each stage was characterized by a unique virtue. The stages are as follows:

Personality Stage	*Virtue*
Trust vs. Mistrust	Hope
Autonomy vs. Shame, Doubt	Willpower
Initiative vs. Guilt	Purpose
Industry vs. Inferiority	Competence
Identity vs. Role Confusion	Fidelity
Intimacy vs. Isolation	Love
enerativity vs. Stagnation	Care
Integrity vs. Despair	Wisdom

On the whole, Erikson's theory broadened the canvas of the psychodynamic theory of Self by incorporating elements of not just sexuality but also society and culture (www.haverford.edu/psych/ddavis/p.109g/erikson.stages.html).[20]

Heinz Kohut, a proponent of the Psychodynamic school of thought, developed the theoretical approach of *Self Psychology*. Born in 1913, Kohut like many other Jews fled Nazi occupation in Vienna, Austria, and settled in Chicago. As a prominent member of the Chicago School of Psychoanalysis, he began to work on Freud's structural theory of the id, ego and super-ego. Over time, he rejected this theory and developed his ideas into a theory of a Tripartite self. According to Kohut, this three-part self can only develop when the needs of one's 'self states' including one's sense of worth and well being, are met with in relationships with others. Thus, unlike Freud's traditional psychoanalytic focus on drives and instincts, Kohut's Self Psychology placed a great deal of emphasis on inter-personal relationships (http://en.wikipedia.org/wiki/Heinz_Kohut).[21]

According to Hall and Lindzey (1985), the phenomenal

field of a human being comprises of both the conscious as well as the unconscious experiences. As further development takes place, a portion of this phenomenal field gets differentiated and emerges as the "self". Carl Rogers believed that human beings are completely integrated at infancy: unified in experience, awareness and communication. He believed that the fissures between the self and experience were a consequence of societal influences and the process of socialization.

According to Ryckman (1993), *self-concept* is the "organized set of characteristics that the individual perceives as peculiar to himself/herself" (http://pandc.ca/?cat=carl_rogers & page=rogerian_theory).[22] Two other significant notions of self are *self-awareness* and *self-consciousness*. Self-awareness is an explicit understanding that one exists and it also includes an awareness of existing as an individual with private thoughts, separate from the others. Self-consciousness on the other hand, is a personal understanding of the very core of one's identity (Ibid).[23]

Identity

Identity is the very core of an individual's sense of self. It is through one's identity that one defines oneself in relation to others. An individual's identity evolves in his/her relations with the surrounding world. According to Northrup, identity operates as a dynamic. She defines the identity dynamic "as the tendency for human beings, individually and in groups, to establish, maintain, and protect a sense of self-meaning, predictability, and purpose"(http://www.colorado.edu/conflict/transform/northrup.htm).[24]

Identity as an entity is always evolving. Every identity has a margin, which defines its exclusivity. This characteristic gives an individual a sense of belonging and an awareness of one's being, in comparison to the other. Identity can refer to both self-identity and group-identity. An individual's self image is shaped by the group he belongs to. The emotional bond that an individual shares with members of his/her group determines the extent to which the individual is likely to identify him/herself as 'I' or 'We' in relation to other members of the group. The social identity of an individual is thus derived from an individual's knowledge of the group as well as the value and emotional significance attached to that membership. The identity of the collective is intrinsically related to the identity of the self. In times of crisis, the collective identity can overwhelm the individual identity as the group can emerge as the primary means of defense.

Social Conflicts

Identity issues fuel most of the *Social Conflicts*. Conflicts can occur when an individual or a group feels that his or her sense of self is being threatened, violated or denied legitimacy. In the face of multiple repressive conflicts, self-preservation becomes a major motivation. The loss of identity, even symbolically, can be devastating for an individual. Identity is the core of an individual and it defines who he/she is. When the identity is attacked upon, it is perceived as a deeper attack on one's self and being. When one realizes the attempts to annihilate one's very core, one chooses to fight back.

In times of crisis, when the identity of an individual or a group is threatened, the insecurity surrounding its very survival can be potent enough to trigger dangerous hostilities within the society. The rigid 'Us' and 'Them' conceptualizations held by each party in conflict, can lead to further divisions and create faultlines within the community. Reciprocal distortion of group images and identities can escalate the tensions and may result in violence. Identity also plays a significant role in the escalation, maintenance and transformation of conflicts.

The social processes of the creation of self and identity are closely intertwined. As individual entities, both *self* as well as *identity* play a significant role in shaping a person's social exchanges in the society. They not only mould an individual's harmonious relationships with others, but also lend form to divergences and differences of opinions, leading to conflicts within the society. The significance of both these entities becomes more apparent in the context of the emerging revivalist trends in the society today.

REFERENCES

1 http://www.thefreedictionary.com/revivalism Accessed on 22/10/06.

2 McLoughlin (Jr.), W.G. (1959). Modern Revivalism: Charles Grandison Finney to Billy Graham. *American Sociological Review,* Volume 24,No.5. New York: Ronald Press Co.

3 Syed, M.A. (2004). *The Position of Women in Islam: A Progressive View*. USA: State University of New York Press.

4 http://columbia.thefreedictionary.com/Islam+(concept) Accessed on 22/10/06.

5 Esposito, J.L &Voll, J.O. (1996). *Islam and Democracy*. New York: Oxford University Press.

6 *Ibid*.

7 *Ibid*.

8 *Ibid*.

9 Wolff, S. (2004). Managing and Settling Ethnic Conflicts In: Wolff, S & Schneckener, U (Eds.). *Managing and Settling Ethnic Conflicts: Perspectives on Successes and Failures in Europe, Africa and Asia*. UK: C. Hurst & Co. Ltd.

10 *Ibid*.

11 http://www.jstor.org/view/00405841/ap050108/05a00050/0 Accessed on 22/10/06.

12 Gahramanova, A (2006). *Identity Conflicts and its Implications for Conflict Management*. UNISCI Discussion Papers, No.11.

13 http://www.skynet.ie/~peacesoc/read/nationmasculinity.html Accessed on 14/09/06.

14 *Ibid*.

15 Gahramanova, A (2006). *Identity Conflicts And Its Implications For Conflict Management*. UNISCI Discussion Papers, No.11.

16 *Ibid*.

17 http://www.psych.neu.edu/ISSI/daily.htm Accessed on 22/09/06.

18 *Ibid.*

19 http://allpsych.com/psychology101/defenses.html Accessed on 15/11/06.

20 http://www.haverford.edu/psych/ddavis/p.109g/erikson.stages.html Accessed on 20/11/06.

21 http://en.wikipedia.org/wiki/Heinz_Kohut Accessed on 22/09/06.

22 http://pandc.ca/?cat=carl_rogers&page=rogerian_theory Accessed on 14/11/06.

23 *Ibid.*

24 http://www.colorado.edu/conflict/transform/northrup.htm Accessed on 3/10/06.

III

WOMEN AND CONFLICT TRANSFORMATION: RETROSPECT AND PROSPECT

Culture of domination provides the framework for oppression. Patriarchy refers to a system of social structures and practices in which men dominate, oppress and exploit women (Miller in Skjelbaek & Smith (Eds.) 2001, p.81).[1] In a patriarchal society, conflicts are envisaged as exclusive domains of masculinity. Wars and armed conflicts are cherished symbols of manhood in the social memories of a community. Women are deprived of a rightful place in these narratives by being relegated to the background as mere objects of support, as peripherals rather than as active agents of change.

For long, gender studies were excluded from the sphere of peace research. This resulted in a skewed presentation of the reality. Statistics reveal that between 1990 and 1999, the world saw 118-armed conflicts and approximately 6 million people were killed. Most of these conflicts were civil wars. It is also believed that unlike the previous decades, almost 75% of all war deaths today are civilian non-combatants (Skjelbaek & Smith, 2001, p .3).[2] This includes a large number of women and children. The fact that women are the easy targets of such conflicts, have been given due recognition in recent research. However their roles as active agents of peacemaking in their communities have not been adequately acknowledged so far.

Peacebuilding

The term Peacebuilding has been variously defined.

Peacebuilding is not just about ending the apparent, visible face of violence but an effort to re-construct the society and usher in a transformation in the social structures that give birth to the violence in the first place.

There are two main theoretical approaches to understand the nature of peacebuilding. First is the *deductive approach* and the second is the *inductive approach*. In the deductive approach, the content of peacebuilding is deduced from the existing capacities and mandates of international organizations. Whereas, in the inductive approach, the content of peacebuilding is determined by the particular matrix of needs and capacities in individual cases (Cousens in Cousens, Kumar and Wermester (Ed.), 2001, p.5).[3] Therefore, while the deductive approach deals more with the content of the conflict, the inductive approach deals with the causes that led to the conflict.

Conflict Transformation

Conflict Transformation includes concepts of both *conflict management and conflict resolution*. Before embarking on the issue of conflict transformation, it is important to understand how it is different from conflict management and conflict resolution.

Conflict Management

According to Bloomfield and Reilly, *Conflict management* is the positive and constructive handling of difference and divergence. Rather than advocating methods of removing conflict, [it] addresses the more realistic question of managing conflict: how to deal with it in a constructive way, how to bring opposing sides together in a cooperative process, how to design a practical, achievable, co-operative system for constructive management of difference (cited in Miall in Wimmer et al., 2004,p.162).[4]

Conflict Resolution

Conflict resolution theorists argue that, "it is possible to transcend conflicts if parties can be helped to explore, analyze, question and reframe their positions and interests. Conflict resolution therefore emphasizes intervention by skilled but powerless third parties working unofficially with parties to foster new ways of thinking and new relationships" (Miall in Wimmer et al., 2004, p.162).[5]

Conflict Transformation

Conflict transformation, on the other hand includes bringing about a structural and relational change within the society to bring a halt to the existing conflict.

Observes, to Ledarach (1995),

> Conflict transformation must actively envision, include, respect and promote the human and cultural resources from within a given setting. This involves a new set of lenses through which we do not primarily "see" the setting and the people in it as the "problem" and the outsider as the "answer." Rather we understand the long-term goal of transformation as validating and building on people and resources within the setting (cited in Miall in Wimmer et al., 2004,p. 163).[6]

According to Galtung, "conflicts have both life-affirming and life-destroying aspects. Once formed, conflicts undergo a variety of transformational processes: articulation or disarticulation, conscientization or deconscientization, complexification or simplification, polarization or depolarization, escalation or de-escalation."(Galtung, 1996 cited in Miall in Wimmer et al., 2004,p. 163).[7]

Theoretical Perspectives of Conflict Transformation

Conflict Theorists have formulated various approaches to conflict transformation. They are as follows:

Vayrynen (1991) has formulated a conflict theory based

on the idea of transformation of conflict. He believes that conflicts are of a dynamic nature. He offers a useful classification of four ways in which conflict can be transformed. "Actor transformations" involve internal transformations in parties and the appearance of new parties. "Issue transformations" involve changes in the issues in conflict and parties' positions on those issues. "Rules transformations" are changes in the norms or rules governing a conflict. "Structural transformations" involve a change in the structure of relations and power distribution of the conflict setting (cited in Miall in Wimmer et al., 2004, p. 165).[8]

Rupesinghe (1995, 1998) devised an approach that integrated conflict resolution training and track-one interventions, including diplomatic interventions and peacekeeping. Ledarach (1997) provided a comprehensive approach on conflict transformation. His theory exemplifies how changes occurring in the various aspects of conflict can impact upon different levels of the system. Structurally, his theory can be represented as a pyramid with elite leaders and decision makers at the top; leaders of social organizations, churches, top journalists, and the like in the middle and grassroots community leaders at the base (cited in Miall in Wimmer et al., 2004, p. 165).[9]

Building on Vayrynen's (1991) approach, Miall has identified five types of transformations or transformers:

- Context transformations: They refer to changes in the context of conflict that may radically alter the conflict situation, or the motives of the parties.
- Structural transformations: They refer to change in the basic structure of conflict, that is, the set of actors, issues and incompatible goals, and conflicting beliefs or relationships, or to the society or state within which the conflict is embedded.

- Issue transformations: They refer to the positions that parties take on key issues at the heart of conflict, and the way that parties redefine or reframe their positions, or reach compromises and resolutions.
- Actor transformations: They include decisions by actors to change goals or alter their approach to conflict, such as decisions to seek peace or initiate a peace process. They also include changes of leadership, which are often crucial in securing transformation in conflicts.
- Personal transformations: They refer to changes of heart and mind in individual leaders or in small groups with decision-making power at critical moments, may be crucial (cited in Wimmer et al., 2004, p.168).[10]

Francis & Guus Meijer have developed a model of conflict transformation, which elucidates the stages that can lead to a transformation of the hostilities in an asymmetrical power context. According to this model, power relations begin to change when those who are oppressed bring their oppression into awareness. This process was termed as 'conscientization' by Paulo Freire (1972). Subsequently, they can mobilize themselves and others for action. Mobilization involves the formation of groups and networks, the articulation of common goals and strategizing about a common line of action. Once they have emboldened themselves and have acquired sufficient leverage, they can act upon their newly found strength and confront their oppressors. The Model is represented in a figure below: (Francis in Austin, Fischer & Ropers (Eds.), 2004, pp. 98-99).[11]

STAGES AND PROCESSES IN CONFLICT TRANSFORMATION

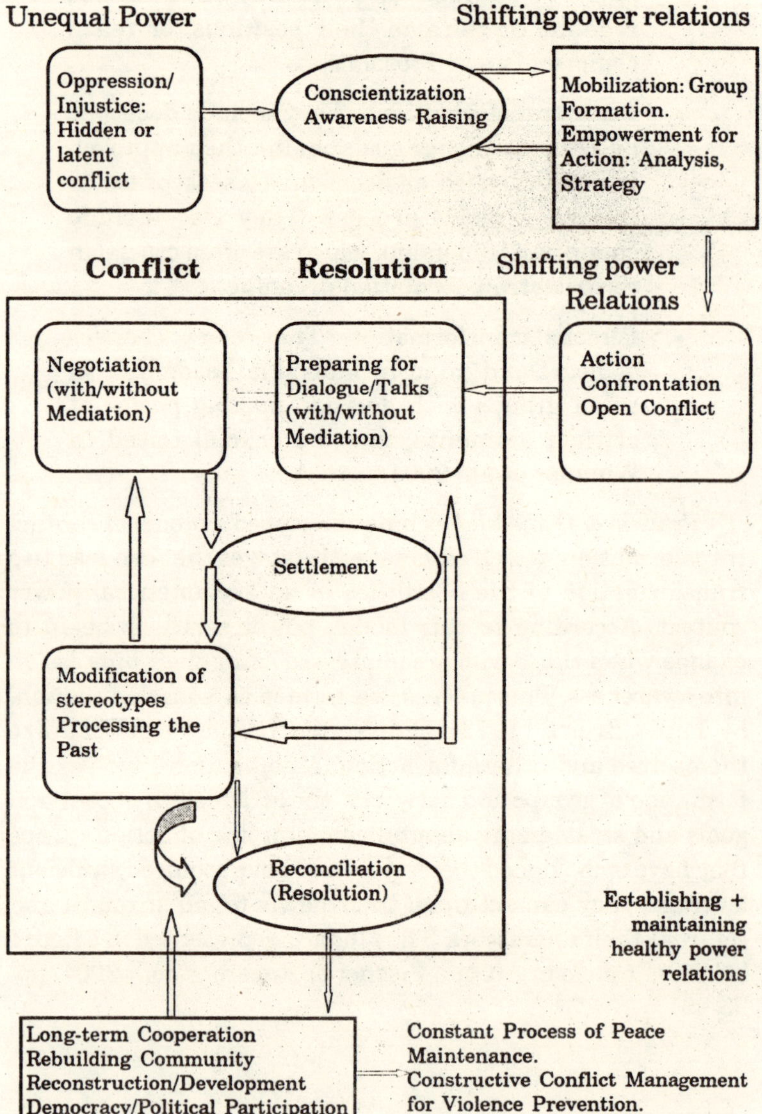

(**Francis & Guus Meijer, 2004**).

Women and Conflict Transformation

In the prevalent patriarchal mindset, women are accepted as cultural symbols and expected to preserve and maintain their cultural traditions. Questions of honour and integrity are tied to their identities and whenever the conflict in the society gets entangled in the questions of identity and ethnicity, the women become subjected to an enormous amount of societal control—their mobility becomes restricted, their privacy is infringed upon and their voices are often silenced.

According to Isabel Coral Cordero, Peacebuilding has to do to with constructing alternative local development models that focus not only on deactivating political and social violence and its consequences, but also, and more importantly on preventing violence by addressing the structural economic, social, political, and cultural inequities that favour its development (Cordero in Moser & Clark (Eds.), 2001, pp. 161-162).[12]

Peacebuilding involves the adoption of strategies that can facilitate and sustain the transition from conflict to sustainable development. The key factor in the peacebuilding process is to sustain an environment of peace and security in an everyday setting.

Women have been found to play an active role in conflict transformation. Their strategies for peacebuilding vary depending on their culture as well as the context of the conflict, and can include among others: forming organizations to campaign for women's rights; resisting war and initiating efforts for peace; working towards developing peace education; initiating post-conflict reconstruction efforts and fostering dialogues between groups in conflict.

Women are often successful in bridging the gap between the grassroots and the powers- that-be. In an environment of turmoil and conflict, women can emerge as active social actors, voicing the concerns of the marginalized population and initiate efforts to rebuild broken communities.

There have been debates regarding the inherent peaceful nature of women and whether they are biologically geared towards peacemaking. Such contestations have mostly been in the realm of the masculinity-feminity debate. Proponents of this debate hold the view that the men are more aggressive, biologically as well as a product of socialization and hence are naturally prone to aggression. They also believe that women are more nurturing and have an inherent maternal instinct in them and are hence more inclined towards peacemaking.

The former Secretary General of the United Nations, Kofi Annan had stated that, "women are always better equipped than men to present or resolve conflict. For generations, women have served as peace educators in their families and societies" (Dutta, 2002, p. 70).[13] In 2000, the United Nations Security Council adopted a landmark resolution on Women and Peace and Security that called for the inclusion of more women in peacekeeping negotiations and peacekeeping forces worldwide, as well as within the U.N. peacebuilding system.

Recommendations of the U.N. Security Council Resolution 1325, adopted by the Security Council at its 4213th meeting on 31 October 2000 are as follows (www.un.org/womenwatch/osagi/pdf/res1325.pdf)[14]:

1) *Urges* member states to ensure increased representation of women at all decision-making levels in national, regional and international institutions and mechanisms for the prevention, management and resolution of conflict;

2) *Encourages* the Secretary-General to implement his strategic plan of action (A/49/587) calling for an increase in the participation of women at decision-making levels in conflict resolution and peace processes.

3) *Urges* the Secretary-General to appoint more women

as special representatives and envoys to pursue good offices on his behalf, and in this regard calls on member states to provide candidates to the Secretary-General, for inclusion in a regularly updated centralized roster;

4) *Further urges* the Secretary-General to seek to expand the role and contribution of women in the United Nations field based operations, and especially among military observers, civilian police, human rights and humanitarian personnel;

5) *Expresses* its willingness to incorporate a gender perspective into peacekeeping operations, and *urges* the Secretary-General to ensure that, where appropriate, field operations include a gender component;

6) *Requests* the Secretary-General to provide to member states training guidelines and materials on the protection, rights and the particular needs of women, as well as on the importance of involving women in all peacekeeping and peacebuilding measures, *invites* member states to incorporate these elements as well as HIV/AIDS awareness training into their national training programmes for military and civilian police personnel in preparation for deployment, and *further requests* the Secretary-General to ensure that civilian personnel of peacekeeping operations receive similar training;

7) *Urges* member states to increase their voluntary financial, technical and logistical support for gender-sensitive training efforts, including those undertaken by relevant funds and programmes inter alia, the United Nations Fund for Women and United Nations Children's Fund, and by the Office of the United Nations High Commissioner for Refugees and other relevant bodies;

8) *Calls* on all actors involved, when negotiating and implementing peace agreements, to adopt a gender perspective, including inter alia:

a) The special needs of women and girls during repatriation and resettlement and for rehabilitation, reintegration and post-conflict reconstruction;

b) Measures that support local women's peace initiatives and indigenous processes for conflict resolution, and that involve women in all of the implementation mechanisms of the peace agreements;

c) Measures that ensure the protection of and respect for human rights of women and girls, particularly as they relate to the constitution, the electoral system, the policy and the judiciary;

9) *Calls* upon all parties to armed conflict to respect fully international law applicable to the rights and protection of women and girls, especially as civilians, in particular the obligations applicable to them under the Geneva Conventions of 1949 and the Protocols thereto of 1967, the Convention on the Elimination of All Forms of Discrimination Against Women of 1979 and the Optional Protocol thereto of 1999 and the United Nations Convention on the Rights of the Child of 1989 and the two Original Protocols thereto of 25 May 2000, and to bear in mind the relevant provisions of the Rome Statute of the International Criminal Court;

10) *Calls* on all parties to armed conflict to take special measures to protect women and girls from gender-based violence, particularly rape and other forms of sexual abuse, and all other forms of violence in situations of armed conflict;

11) *Emphasizes* the responsibility of all states to put an end to impunity and to persecute those responsible for genocide, crimes against humanity, and war crimes including those relating to sexual and other violence against women and girls and in this regard stresses the need to exclude these crimes, where feasible from amnesty provisions;

12) *Calls* upon all parties to armed conflict to respect the civilian and humanitarian character of refugee camps and settlements, and to take into account the particular needs of women and girls, including in their design, and recalls its resolutions 1208 (1998) of 19 November 1998 and 1296 (2000) of 19 April 2000;

13) *Encourages* all those involved in the planning for disarmament, demobilization and reintegration to consider the different needs of female and male ex-combatants and to take into account the needs of their dependants;

14) *Reaffirms* its readiness whenever measures are adopted under Article 41 of the Charter of the UN, to give consideration to their potential impact on the civilian population, bearing in mind the special needs of women and girls, in order to consider appropriate humanitarian exemptions;

15) *Expresses* its willingness to ensure that Security Council missions take into account gender considerations and the rights of women, including through consultation with local and international women's groups;

16) *Invites* the Secretary-General to carry out a study on the impact of armed conflict on women and girls, the role of women in peacebuilding and the gender dimensions of peace-processes and conflict resolution,

and *further invites* him to submit a report to the Security Council on the results of this study and to make this available to all member states of the United Nations;

17) *Requests* the Secretary-General, where appropriate, to include in his reporting to the Security Council, progress on gender mainstreaming throughout peacekeeping missions and all other aspects relating to women and girls;

18) *Decides* to remain actively seized of the matter.

According to McKay and Mazurana, Peacebuilding includes gender-aware and women-empowering political, social, economic, and human rights. It includes personal and group accountability and reconciliation processes that contribute to the reduction/ prevention of violence. It fosters the ability of women, men, girls and boys in their culture (s) to promote conditions of non-violence, equality, justice, and human rights of all people to build democratic institutions and to sustain the environment (www.igw.org/peace/peacebuilding/raising-womens-voices.html).[15]

Speaking about their experiences of working with grassroots organizations involved in post-conflict reconstruction, McKay and Mazurana stated:

> Many NGOs and grassroots groups were found to view peacebuilding as a process, not a product, through which psychosocial, relational and spiritual needs were addressed. Grieving, sharing stories, participating in actions demanding governmental accountability, training in responding to post-traumatic stress disorder at individual and community levels, and working on common projects such as building schools and running radio stations were some of the processes through which communities sought to heal and rebuild communities and build just peace (www.trinstitute.org/ojpcr/3_3rev.htm).[16]

The process of Peacebuilding is critical for the transition from conflict and insecurity to a situation of sustainable peace and development. Women have been found to make a difference in peacemaking because of their inclusive approach towards peace and security. Women's movement for peace can be a force to reckon with in conflict-prone communities, as it can be a powerful interface for effective mediation and building democratic and participatory public institutions.

History of Women's Movement in Egypt

The emergence of the women's movement in Egypt can be traced to the participation of Egyptian women in the revolution of 1919 and the subsequent rise of feminist activism associated with Huda Sha'rawi and the Egyptian Feminist Union (EFU) established in 1923 (Al-Ali, 2002, p.5).[17]

Huda Sha'rawi was born Nur al- Huda Sultan in 1879 at Minya in Upper Egypt. At thirteen years of age, Huda was married off to her cousin and legal guardian, Ali Sha'rawi, under family pressure. She separated from her husband for seven years, when she was fourteen and returned to family life at twenty-one years of age. Huda Sha'rawi was active in the movement for national independence from 1919-1922. In 1923, when Huda Sha'rawi was forty-four, she founded the *al-Ittihad al-Nisa'I al Misri* (the Egyptian Feminist Union) and led a feminist movement until her death in 1947 (Badran, 1996, p.33).[18]

Another lady who sparked the Feminist consciousness of her era was Nabawiyah Musa who rebelled against the authoritarian structures of her time to emerge as a pioneering educator of women. Nabawiyah Musa was born in the town of Zagazig in the province of Qalyubiyah in 1886. She studied in the Girls' Section of the Abbas Primary School and upon graduating in 1906, became a teacher there. In 1907, she petitioned the Ministry of Education to be allowed to sit for the state baccalaureate examination, which until then was permitted only for boys. She prepared for the examinations at home and emerged in the top three. In 1909, she was invited to teach at the Egyptian University's new extracurricular Section for Women. She became the first Egyptian woman principal at the Girl's School in Fayyum and by the dint of her hard work, in 1924, she became the inspector of the girls' schools (Badran, 1996, pp. 38-39).[19]

Nadjes Al-Ali has outlined the evolution of the feminist agenda in the social consciousness of Egyptian society. The Egyptian Feminist Union voiced the concerns of the rights of women. Their agenda incorporated the demands for the political rights of women, changes in the personal status law (especially for controls on divorce and polygamy), equal secondary school and university education, and expanded professional opportunities for women (Al-Ali, 2002, p.5).[20] Besides this organization, the formation of several women's rights based organizations over the years strengthened the foundations of the women's movement for enhanced social, economic and political rights over and above their demands for basic human rights.

In 1948, Doria Shafik formed the *Bint El-Nil* (Daughter of the Nile) group as an initiative to not only demand complete political rights for women, but also encourage literacy programmes, initiate efforts to improve cultural, health, and social services among the poor and enhance mother and child-care. According to Al-Ali, during the 1940s the women's movement moved in different directions, the aristocratic charity-oriented 'ladies of the salon' affiliated with Princess Chevikar; Doria Shafik's *Bint El-Nil*—a mixture of charity, feminist consciousness-raising and political protest; the *Lagnat al-Shabaat* (Committee of Young Women)—founded by Ceza Nabarawi and Inji Aflatoun to revive the fading Egyptian Feminist Union as it attracted "pro-communist women who were prevented by the government from establishing an organization of their own" (Nelson,1996:165); as well as the welfare-and-Islamist oriented Muslim Women's Society created by Zeinab Al-Ghazali (Al-Ali, 2002, pp.5-7).[21]

Successive political regimes in Egypt have shared differing relations with the feminist movement. According to Al-Ali, "Egyptian feminist activism receded under the rule of Gamal Abdel Nasser (1952-1970) as a result of the state's strict monitoring of political activism and the banning of any kind of autonomous organization." But that notwithstanding, women's position took great strides and they were given increased opportunities and rights within the governmental restrictions. Under President Sadat's regime (1970-1981), the women's movement underwent a mixed bag of experiences. There were positive changes in the Personal Status Law for the women as well as better economic opportunities and improved standards of living. In the contemporary context, under President Hosni Mubarak's regime, Egypt is witnessing a re-emergence of the women's movement. According to Ahmed (1992), the re-emergence of women's activism is linked mainly to the continuing battle over the Personal Status Law and taking up of formerly taboo topics such as contraception and clitoridectomy (Al-Ali, 2002, pp. 6-9).[22]

Observes that Sherifa Zuhur, during the 1990's there was a great increase in public debate on feminist issues. For many years, Egypt has witnessed a growing number of women professionals and the appearance of serious literature dealing with gender issues. The principle of female employment has become entrenched and even conservative forces have accepted education and political mobilization for women (http://meria.idc.ac.il/journal/2001/issue1/jv5n1a6.html).[23]

Zuhur also writes that another phenomenon that changed the scenario of the women's movement in Egypt was a spurt of NGOs focusing on women's rights and issues. In 2000, the National Council of Women (NCW) was officially established with the First Lady, Suzanne Mubarak as the president. The Council has set up working groups in the various governates and has engaged in activities working towards the upliftment of women's economic, social and political rights.

History of Women's Movement in Nagaland

The protracted struggle for independence led by the two leading Naga secessionist outfits (NSCN-IM & NSCN-K) have brought about immense destruction and untold misery amongst the people of Nagaland. The sustained conflict as well as Nagaland's proximity to a porous border with Myanmar has led to increasing proportions of youth engaging in alcoholism and drug abuse.

Traditionally, Naga women are known to have played a pivotal role in stopping inter-factional violence through the institution of the *Pukhreila* (Khashim, 1993, cited in Goswami, 2006, p.17).[24] The woman who got married with a man of another village was known as a *Pukhreila*. During the era of headhunting as well as wars, the *Pukhreila* were entrusted with the responsibility of removing the wounded and the dead from the battlefield. They were the only persons who could move freely in times of conflict and disagreement, acting as the conciliator between warring factions. They were ensured complete protection while performing their duties and severe punishment was meted out to anyone who tried to harm them. The Pukhreila were held in high esteem and accorded the same respect and privileges during conflicts as well as during peacetimes. From time immemorial, they have been accorded the socially sanctioned status of a peacemaker. Carrying on with this tradition, women's associations in Nagaland like the Naga Mothers' Association, Dimapur Naga Women's Ho Ho and others are actively engaged in the peace process.

Using the Motherist agenda as an instrument of peacebuilding, the women in Nagaland established the Naga Mothers Association. The women felt that as mothers, they suffered the repercussions of the violent conflict the most. This was because the mothers were holding the community together. So whenever there was an assault on the social fabric of the community, the mothers were the most intensely affected. The need for a common platform to not only voice the concerns of the mothers caught in the conflict between the State and the insurgents but also to combat social evils like alcoholism and drug abuse was acutely felt.

With these objectives in mind, the NMA was established in 1984. Each Naga tribe sent its representatives to the NMA. Neidonuo Angami, one of the founding members, served as a General Secretary of NMA from 1986-1992 and later became its president for two consecutive terms. Under Neidonuo's able leadership, the NMA took great strides and achieved much in their peacebuilding efforts.

Neidenuo Angami launched the 'Shed No More Blood' campaign, which subsequently led to the meeting between various underground groups and NMA, thus providing the former with an opportunity to meet and share the pain and grief of the Naga mothers. Angami represented NMA in various consultations for the peace processes held in Nagaland, Thailand and New Delhi. In her association with the NMA, Angami has also been instrumental in the emergence of several other establishments: the NMA Youth and Women Welfare Organization (1986) to fight drug abuse and trafficking, alcoholism, and HIV/AIDS; Mount Gilead Home (1989), a rehabilitation centre for drug addicts and alcoholics, the first of its kind in India; the NMA HIV/AIDS Care Hospice (2001) and a paper recycling project with the Mount Gilead. (http://www.indiatogether.org/2005/nov/pce-nagaland.htm).[25]

Apart from NMA, another prominent Naga women's organization is the Naga Women's Union of Manipur (NWUM). Although Naga women, like other women of the tribal societies have a relatively better standing in the society in comparison to women elsewhere in India, they are denied their rightful place in organizations such as Naga HoHo, United Naga Council etc. According to Gina Sangkham, President of NWUM "in 1993, during the Naga Week Program in Kohima, the Tangkhul Sanao Long (the Tangkhul Women's Union) initiated that there should be common platform for the Naga women of Manipur. A meeting was held and on 7th January 1994, our group, christened as Naga Women's Union of Manipur, was formed" (http://www.manipuronline.com/Features/August2002/nagawomenunion23_1.htm).[26]

In Nagaland, women's organizations have played a significant role in not only initiating peace efforts in the insurgency-torn state but also made substantial contributions for the economic and social upliftment of women in the society. The women's movement in Nagaland is a strong force to contend with and its involvement in the grassroots has helped it further the cause of the struggle for women's rights.

REFERENCES

1 Miller, E. (2001). Gender, Power & Politics: An Alternative Politics. In: Skjelsbaek, I & Smith, D (Eds.) *Gender, Peace and Conflict*. London, California and New Delhi: Sage Publications.

2 Skjelsbaek, I & Smith, D (Eds.) *Gender, Peace and Conflict*. London, California and New Delhi: Sage Publications.

3 Cousens, E.M. (2001). Introduction. In: Cousens, E.M., Kumar, C &Wermester, K (Eds.) *Peacebuilding as Politics: Cultivating Peace in Fragile Societies*. USA & UK: Lynne Rienner Publishers, Inc.

4 Miall, H. Transforming Ethnic Conflict: Theories and Practices in Wimmer, A, Goldstone, R.J., Horowitz, D, Joras, U & Schetter, C. (2004). *Facing Ethnic Conflicts: Toward a New Realism*. USA: Rowman & Littlefield Publishers, Inc.

5 *Ibid.*

6 *Ibid.*

7 *Ibid.*

8 *Ibid.*

9 *Ibid.*

10 *Ibid.*

11 Francis, D. (2004). Culture, Power Asymmetries and Gender in Conflict Transformation. In: Austin, A, Fischer, M & Ropers, N (Eds.) *Transforming Ethnopolitical Conflict: The Berghof Handbook*. Germany: VS Verlag Fur Sozialwissen schaften

12 Cordero, I.C. Social Organizations: From Victims to Actors in Peace Building in Moser, C.O.N. & Clark, F.C. (2001). *Victims, Perpetrators or Actors? Gender, Armed Conflict and Political Violence*. New Delhi: Kali for Women.

13 Dutta, A (2002). Women in Conflict Situation: A Case Study of Assam. *Journal of Social Change & Development*, Vol. 1, No.1. Guwahati: Omeo Kumar Das Institute of Social Change and Development.

14 http://www.un.org/womenwatch/osagi/pdf/res1325.pdf Accessed on 27/10/06

15 http://www.igw.org/peace/peacebuilding/raising-womens-voices.html Accessed on 27/10/06

16 http://www.trinstitute.org/ojpcr/3_3rev.htm Accessed on 27/10/06

17 Al-Ali, N.S. (2002). *The Women's Movement in Egypt with selected references to Turkey. Civil Society and Social Movements Programme*, Paper No.5. United Nations Research Institute of Social Development.

18 Badran, M. (1996). *Feminists, Islam and Nation: Gender and the Making of Modern Egypt*. Egypt: American University in Cairo Press.

19 *Ibid.*

20 Al-Ali, N.S. (2002). *The Women's Movement in Egypt with selected references to Turkey. Civil Society and Social Movements Programme*, Paper No.5. United Nations Research Institute of Social Development.

21 *Ibid.*

22 *Ibid.*

23 http://meria.idc.ac.il/journal/2001/issue1/jv5n1a6.html Accessed on 29/10/06

24 http://meria.idc.ac.il/journal/2001/issue1/jv5n1a6.html Accessed on 29/10/06

25 Ruivah, K (1993). Social Changes Among The Nagas (Tangkhul) in Goswami, T (2006). *Role of Women as Peace Builders with Special Reference to Nagaland*. Guwahati: Peace Studies, Omeo Kumar Das Institute of Social Change & Development.

26 http://www.indiatogether.org/2005/nov/pce-nagaland.htm Accessed on 10/09/06

27 http://www.manipuronline.com/Features/August2002/nagawomenunion23_1.htm Accessed on 31/10/06.

IV

THE PATH TAKEN: METHODOLOGICAL PERSPECTIVES

The present work has been carried out with an attempt to make a comparative analysis between the conflict situations of two very diverse yet comparable contexts. The ramifications of the revivalist trends in both Egypt and Nagaland have had a visible impact on the mobility and cultural situatedness of women in their respective communities.

The researcher has adopted the qualitative approach of conducting the research and to this end has constructed a semi-structured questionnaire focusing on various issues pertaining to gender and conflict transformation. Due to the paucity of time, the researcher decided to take two case studies of organizations working for women's rights in both Egypt and Nagaland.

The chapter has been divided into two sections. Section I deals with the various theoretical perspectives within which this study has been carried out and Section II deals with an overview of the sample.

Section I

Qualitative Research

In comparison to the better-known Quantitative research methods, the developments of the Qualitative methods of research have been rather delayed. Qualitative research involves an in-depth understanding of human behaviour. Qualitative

Research relies on reasons behind various aspects of behaviour. Simply put, it investigates the why and how of decision-making, as compared to what, where and when of Quantitative Research. Hence, the need is for smaller but focused samples rather than larger and random samples (http://en.wikipedia.org/wiki/Qualitative_research).[1]

Qualitative research methods focus on the meaning of the experiences and seek to go beyond mere numbers. Its methods involve the collection of information from a naturalized setting and subsequently, develop themes and classificatory categories to further the analytical procedure.

The prevalent limitations in the quantitative approach led the social scientists to re-discover the qualitative methods of conducting research. According to Sherman and Reid (1994), there are several reasons for the adoption of the qualitative method of research *vis a vis* the quantitative methods. First, "there was a recognition that the controlled and reductive procedures of quantitative research tended to selectively ignore much of the context of any study and thereby miss significant factors in the situation that more holistic qualitative observation and description might identify." Secondly, it was recognized that, "the study and the analysis of what goes on in the actual process of practice had been shortchanged in favour of measurable outcomes." Thirdly, "a need existed for more knowledge about the interactive and subjective experience of the client in the clinical change process." Fourthly, "the 'bottom line' numbers of quantitative evaluation have tended to denude the findings of much richness and complexity of what goes on and what has been accomplished in any program or intervention." Fifthly, "it became evident to many social work researchers that a need existed to address these shortcomings with a combination and integration of qualitative and quantitative methods" (Sherman & Reid, 1994, p.3).[2]

Qualitative Research involves the detailed descriptions of

characteristics and events and makes use of tools such as observations, interviews and reviews, to collate relevant information. A brief overview of the methods of qualitative research is given below.

Ethnographic Methods

The Ethnographic approach in Qualitative Research has been largely derived from the field of anthropology. According to Sherman and Reid (1994), "the emphasis in this approach has been the immersion in and participant observation of cultures and societies in the naturalistic settings for the purposes of description and understanding"(Sherman & Reid, 1994, p.4).[3] The ethnographer becomes immersed in the culture he/she is studying and becomes an active participant, recording extensive field notes.

Several theorists such as Sands, Weissman and McClelland, have through their anthropological studies shown the relevance of the ethnographic approach to qualitative research. Sands and McClelland especially make a clear distinction between the *etic* and *emic* approaches. According to them, emic approach is called 'internal' or 'domestic', because its perspective is more from the subjective or inside experience of the culture as well as from the persons under study. On the other hand, etic approach is 'external' or 'alien' in that the researcher's perspective is from outside the culture and he/she studies it using a pre-existing system of knowledge or theory about other cultures (Ibid).[4]

Heuristic Methods

This method allows the researcher to study the phenomena in a naturalized setting without altering it. Heineman Pieper proposes the Heuristic paradigm to qualitative research, which allows the researcher to "discover, without primary concern for the constraints of verification and corroboration, through methods that enable further exploration of promising leads and developments in the practice process"(Sherman & Reid, 1994, p.5).[5]

Grounded Theory Methods

Grounded Theory Methods provide a set of strategies for conducting qualitative research. The Grounded Theory approach has been developed by Glaser and Strauss (1967). According to Charmaz, Grounded Theory methods "are a logically consistent set of data collection and analytic procedures aimed to develop theory" (Charmaz, 1995,p.27).[6] According to Sherman and Reid (1994), "It is an approach and set of methods for discovering theories, concepts and hypotheses, and propositions directly from data rather than from a priori assumptions, other research, or existing theoretical frameworks" (Sherman and Reid, 1994, p.6).[7]

Narrative Methods

According to Goswami (2006), "Narratives represent life stories. Stories mould personal identities and construct lives. In Narrative Analysis, the story is the object of its investigation. In narrating their personal experiences, narrators revisit their past, in an attempt to create an ordered mosaic for the listener. Cultures speak through narratives" (Goswami, 2006, p.29).[8]

Case Study Method

Case Study method involves an in-depth study of a particular instance or event. The case study method is used both in naturalistic studies as well as in fieldwork research. According to Stake (1994), there are three types of case studies each with differing purposes. According to him, Researchers conduct Intrinsic Case Studies solely to gain a better understanding of the individual case. The purpose is not to generate theory but to understand a broad issue. The Instrumental Case Study is used to elaborate a theory or gain a better understanding of a social issue. The researcher's primary interest is in learning about the social issue, and the case study merely serves to facilitate that learning. Researchers may also use a Collective Case Study to further their understanding about a social issue or a group of people. They do this by conducting case studies on a group of individuals or cases (Mark, 1996, p.218).[9]

Thematic Analysis:

Thematic Analysis involves focusing on themes and patterns of behaviour. According to Aronson (1994), the first step is to collect the data. From the transcribed conversations, patterns of experiences can be listed. This can come from direct quotes or paraphrasing common ideas. The next step is to combine and catalogue related patterns into sub-themes. Themes are then, pieced together to form a collective picture. Once, the themes are extracted, an argument has to be built defending the theme (www.nova.edu/ssss/QR/BackIssues/QR2-1/aronson.html).[10]

Tools of Qualitative Research Interview

An interview is a conversation between two or more people where questions are asked to obtain information about the interviewee. Interviews can be divided into two rough types:

a) Interviews of assessment.

b) Interviews for information.

An interview may be tightly structured, semi-structured, un-structured, in-depth or conversational. This methodology involves the researcher and the interviewee in a one to one situation and may be quite time consuming. Interviews also involve communication between two or more persons used for purposes such as diagnosis, education and counseling or to obtain information. Interviews may be done in person (face to face), completed by telephone or may involve use of a computer (http://en.wikipedia.org/wiki/Interview).[11]

Structured Interview

Structured Interview is a type of interview in which questions to be asked; their sequence, and detailed information to be gathered are all pre-determined. It is used where maximum consistency between the interviewer and the interviewees is needed. Structured Interviews can be used for a wide range purposes.

Structured Interview, also known as a Standardized Interview or a Researcher-Administered Survey, is a quantitative research method commonly employed in survey research. The aim of this approach is to ensure that each interviewee is presented with exactly the same questions and this ensures that answers can be reliably aggregated. Structured Interviews are essentially statistical surveys, where the survey is delivered by an interviewer rather than being self-administered (like a questionnaire). The choice of answers to the questions is often fixed (close-ended) in advance. (http://en.wikipedia.org/wiki/Structured_interview).[12]

Semi Structured Interview

This type of an interview involves both closed questions for collecting straightforward data as well as some open-ended questions, which allow the respondent to explain more complex feelings, attitudes and emotions about a concerned topic.

In this study, the researcher has made use of the Case Study method of Qualitative Research and has constructed a semi-structured questionnaire pertaining to the issues listed in the stated objectives.

Section II

Owing to the paucity of time as well as the limitation posed by the language barrier, the researcher chose to restrict the sample size to two case studies: one in Egypt and the other in Nagaland, India. The inherent logic was to choose organizations that were working in the field of women's rights amidst the prevalent situations of conflict in the respective contexts.

Even though the nature of conflict is completely different in both Nagaland as well as in Egypt, it has been seen that organizations championing the cause of women's rights have been toiling endlessly in the face of a multitude of challenges posing before them, whether it be the strict censorship of State authority or the ever-increasing tide of revivalist trends.

In Egypt, the researcher selected the Egyptian Centre for Women's Rights (ECWR) whereas, in Nagaland, the researcher opted for an organization named Prodigals' Home. The aim was to study the strategies adopted by these organizations in the face of the limitations imposed by the revivalists (ethno-centric revivalism in Nagaland and religious revivalism in Egypt) on the women's space and mobility and to explore deeper into the present status of the women (political, economic and social) in both the contexts.

Brief introductions of the organizations are as follows:

Egyptian Centre for Women's Rights (ECWR)

The Egyptian Centre for Women's Rights (ECWR) is a Cairo based independent non-governmental organization that was established in April 1998. The Centre is an advocacy-based organization and carries out programmes and projects at the grassroots level, which aim to enhance the political and human status of women and confront all forms of discrimination against them. A few of its programmes have been as follows:

1. To provide legal aid to women.
2. Support the political rights of women.
3. Cadre School Programme.
4. Capacity Building of local NGOs.
5. To provide access to basic services through Registration.

The ECWR aims at the following:

- Spreading awareness of women's' rights as an integral part of human rights.
- Developing women's rights to participation in public life, particularly the right to vote and run in the elections. In this regard, the Centre seeks to help women register in electoral records and to practice the right to vote. It also seeks to provide women candidates with the skills they need to run in the elections.
- Providing legal assistance to women by bringing lawsuits on their behalf, and getting the court decisions implemented, particularly for women who cannot afford legal expenses. It also provides legal counsel to women.
- Monitoring violations and aggressions against women, whether by individuals, governmental or non-governmental bodies, and making reports to be released to the public outlining the steps necessary to stop these violations.
- Monitoring the laws and legislation that restrict women's rights and do not comply with the Egyptian Constitution and international standards, as well as holding discussion sessions and workshops about these laws to find ways to challenge and amend them.

Prodigals' Home

Prodigals' Home is a Dimapur (in Nagaland) based organization with its area of operation covering the entire Northeastern region of India. It was established in 1990 and was set up to address the rising incidence of drug addiction in Nagaland. Since then, the organization has diversified its areas of operations and incorporated within its fold the larger community issues of strengthening the invaluable traditional institutions, human resource development, natural resource management, women's empowerment and advocacy.

Activities

The activities taken up by the organization depend on the projects undertaken by it. The wide range of activities taken by it is as follows:

Women's Empowerment

- Short Stay Home for women in difficult situations wherein vocational training is imparted and Integrated Growth activities are carried out.
- Self Help Groups for Women are set up for the all round development of women.
- Programmes are also undertaken to focus on female school dropouts.

Prevention and Awareness of HIV/AIDS:

- Awareness to students through SIDU
- Condom promotion/ distribution to Injected Drug Users (IDUs), Commercial Sex Workers and other vulnerable groups.
- NSEPs for IDUs.
- Referral services.
- Information, Education and Communication (IEC) campaign.

Drug Abuse Prevention Programme:

- Detoxification Centre.
- Rehabilitation and after-care centre.
- Drop in Centre (DIC).
- Detox and Counselling camps.
- Campaigns against substance abuse.

- Out-Reach work

Street Children:

- Out-Reach
- Drop in Centre (DIC).
- Treatment, Counselling and Referrals.
- Information dissemination, IEC development, HIV/AIDS, STD (Sexually Transmitted Diseases), STI (Sexually Transmitted Infections) and Drug awareness programmes.

Youth Development Programmes:

- Award of lump sum scholarship.
- Vocational training.
- Initiation of volunteers.
- Recreational activities.

Rural Development:

- Formation of Self Help Groups for Integrated Growth.
- Sustainable Land Management through horticulture.
- Agricultural Storage Shed.
- Vermicompost Units.
- Promotion and marketing of rural products.

Environmental Programmes:

- Sensitization
- Conservation of forest
- Advocating organic farming.

Thus, by taking these case studies, the researcher seeks to explore the dynamic interplay between the movement for women's rights, policies of the state and the emerging revivalist trends in the complex socio-political terrain of Nagaland and Egypt. The researcher hopes to collate data from interviews with key personnel from these organizations and supplement it, with documentation regarding the objectives, policies and programmes of the organization.

REFERENCES

1 http://en.wikipedia.org/wiki/Qualitative_research Accessed on 3/11/06

2 Sherman, E & Reid, W.J. (1994). Introduction: Coming of Age in Social Work—The Emergence of Qualitative Research. In: Sherman, E & Reid, W.J. (Eds). *Qualitative Research in Social Work*. New York: Columbia University Press.

3 *Ibid.*

4 *Ibid.*

5 *Ibid.*

6 Charmaz, K. (1995). Grounded Theory. In: Smith, J.A., Rom Harre' and K.V. Lagenhove (Eds.). *Rethinking Methods in Psychology*, London: Sage Publications.

7 Sherman, E & Reid, W.J. (1994). Introduction: Coming of Age in Social Work—The Emergence of Qualitative Research. In: Sherman, E & Reid, W.J. (Eds). *Qualitative Research in Social Work*. New York: Columbia University Press.

8 Goswami, T (2006). *Role of Women as Peace Builders With Special Reference to Nagaland*. Guwahati: Peace Studies, Omeo Kumar Das Institute of Social Change and Development.

9 Mark, R. (1996). *Research Made Simple: A Handbook for Social Workers*. London, Delhi & U.SA: Sage Publications.

10 http://www.nova.edu/ssss/QR/BackIssues/QR2-1/aronson.html Accessed on 9/11/06

11 http://en.wikipedia.org/wiki/Interview Accessed on 9/11/06

12 http://en.wikipedia.org/wiki/Structured_interview Accessed on 13/11/06

V

A CLOSER LOOK: ANALYSIS AND DISCUSSION

Revivalist trends have swept over the socio-political landscape of both Nagaland and Egypt, transforming the social fabric of the communities. They have also induced changes within the social structure thereby placing the women at a greater risk. Besides their individual revivalist movements, both Nagaland and Egypt are wrought with specific social realities of their own.

NAGALAND

Nagaland has been home to the longest guerilla movement in India. The revivalist movement here has taken an ethnic hue. Over the years, the revivalists have scaled down their demands from outright secessionism from the Indian Union to an integration of Naga inhabited areas, *Nagalim,* in the Northeastern region of India. As the ethnic revivalists are waging an armed struggle against the Indian Union, the movement has grown into a full-fledged, low intensity insurgency. Compounding to this state of affairs, are several other difficulties plaguing the society. The insurgency as well as the porous international borders have led to an increase in the incidence of drug trafficking, drug abuse, HIV/AIDS, commercial sex workers and other associated repercussions such as broken homes, single mothers, domestic violence etc.

A complex situation such as this exposes the women in the region to a wide-ranging set of problems. The low intensity armed conflict in Nagaland has led to the presence of large companies of the armed forces (the India Army and various other paramilitary forces). Consequently, women's spaces and mobility have become highly restricted. Porous international borders provide for an easily available market for flesh trade. Caught in the complex vortex of such a socio-political scenario, women emerge as vulnerable victims.

Amidst this rather disappointing scenario, women have both individually as well as collectively, spearheaded movements for change. They have set up organizations in rural as well as urban areas to address the various issues plaguing the society. These organizations serve as platforms to embody the voice of the collective. The Naga Mothers Association and Dimapur Naga Women's Hoho are the most common names that come to the mind. Other than these, there are several organizations set up to meet the needs of the community. One such organization, also taken as a case study, is *Prodigals' Home,* based in Dimapur, Nagaland.

Prodigals' Home

Prodigal's Home came into existence in the year 1990. It was set up to address the rising incidence of drug addiction in the state, which affected every household at that time. Since then, the organization has consistently campaigned for a drug-free society. Over the years, the organization has moved on to larger community issues of strengthening the invaluable traditional institutions, human resource development, natural resource management, women's empowerment and advocacy.

EGYPT

The Arab Republic of Egypt has witnessed the successive change of political regimes over the years. The differing ideological leanings of the political regimes have shaped and impacted upon the dynamics between the state and the revivalists. The revivalist movement in Egypt has taken on a religious hue. Over the years, there has been an increase in religious conservatism with its most visible manifestation in the rising incidences of veiling. The phenomenon of veiling is visible not only amongst the women of the older generation but also amongst the youth.

In her interactions with the women in Egypt, the researcher found that there were three categories of veiled women. First, women in the *hijab*, a cloak that covered the lady from head to toe. Secondly, women in the *niqab*, a cloak covering the entire body along with a face veil, with only the eyes visible and thirdly, women dressed in western outfits but with a headscarf. Headscarves were also worn in a variety of ways. Some were worn tightly around the head and pinned underneath the neck, while others wore it loosely and tied it around the hair bun at the nape of the neck. Egyptian markets had rows of shops dedicated to scarves alone, in different materials...from silk to chiffon, sequined, embroidered and in as many colours and designs as one could imagine! Not all women were veiled in Egypt though. Besides the minority Coptic Christian population, there were many others professing Islam who had decided not to don the veil for personal reasons.

As in Nagaland, in Egypt too, the women have had to bear the brunt in the conflict between the State and the revivalists. Other than the pressure on the women to don the veil, several other issues concerning the women, such as female genital mutilation (FGM), abortion, early marriage and right to work, have been embroiled in the complex dynamics between the state and the revivalists. In all of this, the women get enmeshed in the social quagmire.

Although the State has adopted several women friendly laws through legislation, loopholes within have prevented their thorough application on the ground. According to Mona Zulficar, an international lawyer and a human rights activist,

> On one hand, the majority of laws in Egypt have provided for equal opportunities and equality before

> the law, without any discrimination against women. However difficulties were encountered in the application of these laws on grounds of social, cultural and economic constraints and prevailing traditions and social conditions. Affirmative action is therefore warranted, particularly with respect to the application of laws on education, health, employment and political rights. Moreover strategies to increase women's awareness of their legal rights and encourage exercise of such rights should be developed and implemented (www.ecwronline.org/english/researches/index.htm).[1]

Despite these complexities, several women have initiated movements of change in Egypt, both at the individual as well as collective levels. Several organizations have sprung up fighting for the cause of women, taking up the cudgels against discriminatory laws and voicing the grievances of the voiceless and marginalized women. Mention may be made of the National Council for Women, Arab Women's Solidarity Association, Egyptian Centre for Women's Rights and Alliance for Arab Women etc. The Egyptian Centre for Women's Rights (ECWR), a Cairo based organization, has been taken as a case study for this project.

Egyptian Centre for Women's Rights (ECWR)

The Egyptian Centre for Women's Rights is a Cairo based independent non-governmental organization that was established in April 1998. The Centre carries out programmes and projects at the grassroots level, which aim at enhancing the political and economic status of women and confront all forms of discrimination against them. Through its programmes, the Centre attempts to help enable the women to obtain their legal rights, offer legal and family counselling as well as monitor the violations inflicted on women. The Centre also carries out programmes that encourage and empower women to participate in political life through different means (for example, registration of names, voting, running for elections etc). The

Centre's programmes cover both rural as well as urban areas of Egypt.

The Interviews taken with Ms. Nehad Abul Komsan (ECWR) and Ms. K. Ela (Prodigal Home) as well as with other individuals have revealed several significant themes revolving around the dynamic relations shared between the State and the revivalists and the situatedness of women between these two entities. For the sake of clarity, this chapter has been divided into three sections. Section I deals with the themes that are common for both the contexts. Section II deals with the prospects and concerns of the Women's Movement in both Nagaland and Egypt and finally, Section III deals with issues specific to both the contexts.

Section I

Egyptian Centre for Women's Rights (ECWR) and Prodigal Home (PH) are both woman headed organizations, working on social issues and issues concerning women. Experiencing a lacuna in their respective social contexts both organizations were driven to make their presence felt.

Prodigal Home was set up in 1990 to counter the increasing incidence of drug addiction in Nagaland. According to K. Ela, the present Director of Prodigal Home,

> "In the late 1980s and 1990s, the incidence of drug addiction had increased manifold in the state. Prodigal Home was set up by the founder Director to address this problem. Over the years, it expanded its area of operation to include Injected Drug Users (IDU) and male drug users. Today, it also works with male and female drug users, sex workers, street and slum children etc. The organization also runs a Short Stay Home for women and girls who need a place to stay."[2]

ECWR was established keeping in mind not only the prevalent discriminatory laws against women but also the lack of political and civil rights of women in Egypt. According to Nehad A. Komsan.

> After the International Conference on Population and Development held in Cairo in 1994, legislations for women were reviewed for the first time. The conference brought a lot of issues to the forefront and several significant issues were discussed on a public platform. The review of the available legislations also revealed the discriminatory policies towards women. At that time, we realized the need for an organization that could provide legal assistance to the women. We use direct assistance as an instrument to understand the legislation better. It is a practical approach and we focus on the grassroots. They teach us more than we teach them (referring to working with women at the grassroots).[3]

Projects and Programmes for Women

Both ECWR and Prodigal Home have definite programmes for women— Initially set up to work with Injected Drug Users, Prodigal Home has over the years, expanded its areas of operation to include female drug users, sex workers, street and slum children. It also runs a Short Stay Home for women and girls. The inmates are sent to other centres for vocational training while skills like basket weaving and needlework are taught in the organization itself. Once trained, the women are incorporated within the organization. The organization also focuses on female school dropouts. It tries to address problems concerning women in rural areas, such as encouraging the habit of saving and formation of SHGs. To improve the economic condition of the women, training on organic kitchen garden and community gardens are encouraged, so that through shared labour, they could earn profits.

Egyptian Centre for Women's Rights is basically an advocacy-based organization. It is not a charitable or a service-oriented organization. It is a centre promoting the legal and political rights of women. Its aim is to assist women to get empowered. According to Ms. Nehad A. Komsan,

> The absence of women in high levels of decision-making, made us realize the need to groom women in leadership skills and the dire need for the political empowerment of women. The main thrust of ECWR is human rights: to raise women's awareness as human rights. When we first established ECWR in 1996, we decided to focus on women who were not registered at birth. We decided to take one village as a case study and reveal to the people what it entailed to be without *birth certificates*. Having no birth certificates meant being out of record. Being out of the official records meant being deprived of state policies and benefits like pensions, subsidies for medical treatment, education, jobs and the entire gamut of developmental programmes.[4]

She mentioned that initially no one perceived this as a problem but they took it upon themselves to convey to the various governmental departments in a language they could understand. To try and make people understand the magnitude of the problem, they tried to interpret it in a manner they could understand better. They told the politicians and the political parties that they were missing out on a vote bank and as rightful citizens of the country, these people should be given electoral cards to exercise their right to vote. To the Ministry of Interior, it was conveyed that people who were out of the records could pose to be a security scare and could be bad for the overall security of the nation. To the Ministry of Health, it was told that unless they knew about the total population of a place, they could not effectively implement their policies and programs and would more often than not, face the ire of the people for their ineffectiveness. Thus the attempt of creating a language that people understood went a long way in helping the people take this problem seriously and acknowledge it as a reality in the current context.

With regards to the issue of *Female Genital Mutilation* (FGM) and the issue of *Early Marriages*, Ms. Komsan stated,

> We try to take it up from a legal standpoint and try to relate to it from the people's point of view. Our experience has shown that when we discuss it with villagers, they say that they practice FGM because they want to protect their daughters. They also believe that getting their daughters married off early could ensure a good life for them. So ECWR decided to work for the education of the girls. In Egypt, till 18 years of age, education is free and in primary school the annual fee is about 8 dollars. So we took the matter up with the Ministry of Education to see if this annual fee could be reduced.[5]

Difficulties faced by the organizations from the revivalists

The interviews with the Directors of the two organizations have revealed that other than the subtle warnings issued by the revivalists regarding the accepted form of dress code for women, there have been no clashes with the revivalists on any matter. In the case of Nagaland, interviews with Ms. K.Ela (of Prodigal Home) and Pastor Dirang Lungalang[6], have revealed that about two years ago, a certain faction of the revivalists had issued a *diktat* demanding that women dress more conservatively. But subsequently, due to massive public opposition, not much came off this *diktat*. On the other hand, in Egypt, there has been a rise in conservatism, with a visible manifestation of increasing incidences of women donning the *hijab* and the headscarf.

Yet, in both these contexts, it is significant to note that the organizations have been successful in cultivating a positive relationship with the revivalists and in utilizing them to their advantage. Commenting on the relationship with the ethnic revivalists in Nagaland, Ms. K. Ela stated, "We have not faced any problem with them. This is because, they also have rehabilitation centres run by them catering to their cadres addicted to drugs. They send people to our organization to be trained. So we can actually share a bond with them on the drug issue."[7]

On the other hand, with regard to the relationship with the religious revivalists in Egypt, Ms. Nehad A. Komsan stated, "We are not facing any problem from the *fundamentalists*. From Islamists, we face lots of funny issues. We use religious language to prove our point. We use traditions, because we know all traditions are not good and all are not bad. We work with both mosques and churches."

Obstacles faced by the Organization

Working in complex environments, the organizations, however, have had to face several difficulties from different quarters. K. Ela of *Prodigal Home*, stated, That althoufht there has been no apparent opposition or obstacles faced by the organization, it existed in a subtle way. As Prodigal Home works on issues such as drug abuse and HIV/AIDS, it often comes into loggerheads with the Church. Nagaland has a predominant Christian population and the Church is looked upon as an all encompassing, socio-religious entity. Elaborating on it further, she observed.

> There are a lot of problems between NGOs and the Church condemning pre-marital and extra-marital sex. To counter the increasing incidence of HIV/AIDS, the NGOs encourage condom usage for safe sex, while the churches encourage abstinence as the only way to counter it. Churches are also realizing that not every one can abstain and that by encouraging the use of condoms, the NGOs are not increasing the incidence of promiscuity. But we still have a long way to go. We have to educate them on this issue to help them understand that we are not promoting promiscuity.[8]

Elaborating or the obstacles faced by *ECWR*, stated the following,

> Nehad A. Komsan first, we have a dictatorial regime and women's issues are not the foremost on the list of priority issues. If at all, it is the least. Secondly, there is an unhealthy, hidden coalition between political

> Islamists and the Government. It is what I call the Heaven-Devil alliance. Political Islamists through their religious efforts try to make people invisible from the political landscape and not question the government. The Government is fully aware of this and allows it to happen. They allow the Political Islamists, to metaphorically speaking, 'drug the people to sleep' but they also have the ultimate say, in that they prevent them (i.e. the Political Islamists) from emerging as the all powerful...and exercise restraint when necessary. Thirdly, our rich, tolerant traditional culture has become increasingly polluted by the Azhar traditions. In fact, through their efforts they are trying to make bad traditions, a holy issue. Fourthly, the economic situation that is prevalent. Fifthly, there is an awful law controlling the NGOs in the country. Sixthly, we have NGOs and activists but no organized, joint movement per se. The CEDAW Shadow report was a successful effort by different NGOs and activists, but the same cannot be said about the Beijing+5 Platform. Seventhly, the shortage of funds from the Government for the NGOs is a big obstacle. For any funds to come in, there needs to be an approval from the State security and this makes the circle quite tight.

The above clearly shows that in both the contexts, the organizations have to work amidst plenty of hindrances.

Women between the State and the Revivalists

In the complex dynamics between the State authorities and the revivalists, in both Nagaland and Egypt, women have had to bear the brunt.

In Nagaland, the ethnic revivalists are waging an armed struggle against the Indian Union. This has resulted in the presence of huge, standing forces of armed personnel in Nagaland to counter the growing insurgent activities. The women are subjected to violence (both physical as well as psychological), not only from the stationed armed force personnel but also from the armed insurgents. Besides that, the presence of these personnel in large numbers has also spawned demands for flesh trade. Women from poverty stricken backgrounds are easily sucked into these activities and subsequently a ready market for commercial sex work (CSW) has emerged. Being witness to over fifty years of armed struggle has left deep scars in the psyche of the women in Nagaland. Women's mobility has been severely restricted and spaces have been gendered.

Porous international borders and incessant armed struggles have brought about an inflow of drugs and sex trafficking. This has resulted in the increasing incidences of drug abuse and HIV/AIDS. The ever-increasing presence of Injected Drug Users amongst the youth has also raised the numbers affected by AIDS. With drug abuse and AIDS, comes not only death but also a slow deterioration of the social fabric. Families begin to wither away, domestic violence is on the rise and children begin to grow up in broken homes. Women are the worst affected and are often the sole surviving member, trying to weave together a life out of the broken pieces.

Egypt, on the other hand, has witnessed the successive change of political regimes. With the change in the political set up, the relations with the religious revivalists have also undergone transformations. The complex relations between the State authorities and the religious revivalists have had an effect on the fundamental issues concerning the women as well as the state policies relating to these issues.

According to Nehad A. Komsan, as an organization working for women, ECWR has had to face several problems from the State authorities.

> The main problem we face is in terms of *State Security.* It is easy to work on people's stomach. But once you ignite people's minds, then it could create problems for the state. They cancelled ECWR's Women's Day Celebration because they heard that around 1000 women were supposed to come. Censorship through

> State Security is basically in the form of canceling activities; non-approval of funds for projects and terrorizing staff. Igniting minds to question the policies and advocate for better education, health, electricity etc. can be frightening for the state authorities. The Government prefers to keep people ignorant, as they are scared that more informative as well as politically aware people can oust them from power. When we worked with the villagers, we tried to help them question the role of the Local Council. Many of them didn't even know what the Local Council or an election was. We had to ask them, when was the last time your wall was dirtied by sticking pictures or bills...that was the local council elections. An ironical incident but it also reveals the extent of ignorance of the people at the grassroots, who are not only deprived of their rightful status but also excluded from the participatory political process.[9]

Besides censorship from state authorities, the *rise in conservatism* has also added to the woes of women in Egypt. With a strong wave of religious revivalism, issues such as Female Genital Mutilation (FGM), early marriage, birth control, veiling, right to work etc. get entangled in the complex socio-political debates. Elaborating on the issue of rise in conservatism in Egypt, Komsan observed.

> The reason for the rise in conservatism in Egypt today is mainly political. Egypt was under British occupation. In 1952, the people's revolution took place. Before the Revolution, politically, Egypt was very liberal. During the 50s and the 60s, the Communist forces came to power. The Communist party was against the multi-party system. When Nasser came to power, Egypt began to look up...politically and socially. Egypt won the war with Israel. There was industrialization and things were looking up. People felt that they had money. Women were elected as Ministers and Ambassadors under his regime. Therefore people felt victorious. When Sadat came to power, people couldn't acknowledge him as their leader and for long accepted him as Nasser's shadow. Just after the Revolution, about 4 million Egyptians went to Saudi Arabia for work.

> When they came back, they returned not only with more monetary wealth accrued from the oil industry but also conservative ideas regarding Islam. This was because, the most conservative school of thought in Islam, the *Wahabi ideology,* has its origins in Saudi Arabia. Anwar Sadat, tried to win over the political Islamists to his side and thus, chose to forge an alliance with the Muslim Brotherhood. During those years, there were several attempts by the Brotherhood to impose through religious ideology their views on FGM and early marriages. Now, nearly 30 years after it all begun, it has begun bearing fruits. Conservatism has increased manifold and has become a visible force in the Egyptian society. The *Wahabi ideology* has made Islam a 'cosmetic rather than a value issue'. When you mix religion and politics, you tend to destroy both. The Egyptian culture actually is very peaceful and very tolerant. The influence of the Coptic tradition can also be seen in many of our traditional practices, especially in agriculture. Al Azhar, which is regarded in high esteem by the Sunni community, is increasingly coming under the influence of the finances of Saudi Arabia, thus implying that the clout of the *Wahabi* school is increasing, thus making it a haven for ultra-conservatives.[10]

The increasing revivalist trend has its most visible manifestation in the rising prevalence of women, both young and old, donning the veil. During her stay in Alexandria, the researcher found a growing consciousness among the youth of their identity and their need to assert it. In the backdrop of the post 9/11 political turmoil, this was probably an expected change amongst the youth of a community that has been increasingly facing marginalization from the international community at large.

Role of Religious Bodies

In both Nagaland and Egypt, the religious bodies namely, the Church in Nagaland and the Mosque and Church in Egypt, have played a considerable role by their presence in the socio-political landscapes.

In Nagaland, the Church and the NGOs are fighting together in their campaign to counter the menace of Drug abuse and HIV/AIDS. The Church is also trying to initiate a dialogue with the armed ethnic revivalists to give up arms and embrace the path of peace. In a recent consultative session held with the National Socialist Council of Nagalim I-M, the Nagaland Baptist Church Council (NBCC) appealed to the leaders to not use the phrase "Nagaland for Christ" till they denounced all violent activities and inter-factional clashes and adopt the path of peace.

In Egypt, ECWR has tried to engage the Church and the Mosque within their fold of activities. According to Komsan, "We use religious language to prove our point. We use traditions, because we know all traditions are not good and all are not bad. We work with both mosques and churches". On June 7-8, 2006, ECWR along with partners from six African countries and the U.K. met in Egypt to prepare a plan to fight FGM and Early Marriage at the *International Conference on FGM and Early Marriage from Religious and Legal perspectives*. 130 public figures including legal professionals, politicians and Islamic and Christian religious authorities, NGOs, journalists, and activists attended the conference from 21 countries. This illustrates how an attempt was made by ECWR to bridge the gap and initiate a dialogue with the religious bodies, so that they too could voice their opinions on issues that concerned women.

Section II

This section will deal with the Women's Movement—its issues and prospects, in both Nagaland and Egypt.

In Egypt, the women's movement can be traced to the participation of women in the 1919 revolution and the subsequent rise of feminist activism associated with activists such as Huda Sha'rawi and the Egyptian Feminist Union (EFU) founded in 1923. The EFU's feminist agenda called for political rights for women, changes in the personal status law, equal secondary school and university education and expanded professional capacities for women (Al-Ali, 2002, p.5).[11]

According to some theorists, the women's movement witnessed a spurt of growth between 1945 and 1959. This period saw the birth of several organizations championing the cause of women. Mention may be made of the *Bint El-Nil* founded by Doria Shafik, *Muslim Women's Society* founded by Zeinab Al-Ghazali and *Lagnat al-Shabaat* founded by Ceza Nabarawi and Inji Aflatoun (Al-Ali, 2002,pp. 6-7).[12]

The state authorities have generated varying discourses on women's rights over the years. As political regimes underwent changes, so did the prevalent dominant discourses on state policies regarding women's issues. This scenario is further complicated by the role of the Islamists. The relations shared between the government and the Islamic Revivalists have shaped the development of the women's movement in a multitude of ways.

Elaborating on the women's movement in Egypt, Komsan affirmed that there had been an absence of a women's movement since the 1950's. The 1960s and 70s saw the emergence of several noted women's activists but no organized movement. On the question of interaction between the women's rights and feminist movement, Komsan acknowledged that the issues were not clearly defined in both and that they tended to often overlap. For nearly fifty years, there have been a number of women's activists, but no women's movement per se. Besides she added, the term 'women's movement', was a broad term and connoted several things at once.[13]

Ms. Komsan believed that the main aim of the women's movement should be the capacity building of the NGOs and the activists. According to her, "once that achieved and the fear from the state security is broken down, a lot more get done. Technical expertise is no doubt required, but more important than that is to *empower the people and make strategic plans for the future.*[14]

She further elaborated:

> Building self-confidence of the women is the first step. It is important to *help her build vision*. ECWR has Small Initiative Programmes for women. A fixed amount of money is given as an endowment to a woman who comes with an idea to market it. The money is given in installments and it is not demanded back by ECWR. The programme is solely dependent on the original ideas of the women and their acumen to market the product. I feel that programmes must be context specific...the same programme need not be successful everywhere. For example, I personally feel that the *Grameen Bank* concept should not have been replicated everywhere, it led to the destruction of moral values creating violence and hatred. I believe that the ideas should come from the women themselves as they know their communities best."[15]

In Nagaland, women have since ancient times been accorded the role of a peacemaker. As mentioned earlier, traditionally, Naga women are known to have played a pivotal role in stopping inter factional violence through the institution of the *Pukhreila* (Khashim, 1993, cited in Goswami, 2006, p.17).[16]

Being witness to a long protracted armed struggle, women in Nagaland have untiringly initiated efforts for peace. Carrying on the mantle of peacemaking, women in Nagaland have organized themselves on several fronts—in urban centres as well as in the grassroots to take forward the message of peace and reconciliation. Women's associations in Nagaland like the Naga Mothers' Association, Dimapur Naga Women's Ho Ho and others are actively engaged in the peace process.

Elaborating on the women's movement in Nagaland, K. Ela stated, "I cannot say that there is a movement *per se.*

although there have been improvements in the scenario over the ages."[17] She felt that the setting up of a State Women's Commission in Nagaland is indeed a great step forward and will go a long way in furthering the movement for women's rights. She believed that women in Nagaland have far from achieved an equal status with men and this was because issues were not being looked through the Rights perspective.

On the question of the future of the women's movement in Nagaland, K. Ela observed:

> An issue of much concern is domestic violence. It is prevalent but women seldom come out to report cases. Awareness needs to be brought about on the issue...even on the Bill on Domestic Violence that has been passed in the Parliament. Most women are not even aware of their rights. The violence will continue until women are made aware of their rights and sensitized on the issue. *Awareness and Sensitization are most significant. Only then, can change come.*[18]

It is thus seen that in both the contexts, the interviewees noted the absence of a women's movement *per se* although women's activists at an individual as well as a collective level, have been furthering the cause of women's rights in both Nagaland and Egypt.

Section III

This section will deal with the issues that are specific to each of the contexts and whose presence amplifies the already existent conflicts.

Nagaland

In Nagaland, the armed struggle for over half a century has brought with it not only immense physical destruction, but also significant social and emotional breakages in the community at large. As mentioned earlier the conflict between the armed ethnic revivalists and the Indian Union has resulted in the presence of large numbers of armed personnel in

Nagaland. The ongoing conflict besides creating an atmosphere of fear, has fuelled a vicious cycle of social ills such as drug abuse, drug trafficking, HIV/AIDS, violence against women (physical as well as emotional), commercial sex work, sex trafficking etc.

Women are caught in the conflict between the State and the Non-State actors. As Roshmi Goswami has stated, "women in situations of conflict are especially impacted upon because of their status in society and their sex and basically all violations can be underpinned to unequal power relations between men and women and the patriarchal attempts of domination and subjugation to perpetrate this inequality"(Goswami, 2000, p.5).[19] In Nagaland, this is clearly reflected in how women get entangled in the crossfire between the state maintained armed forces and the armed ethnic revivalists.

With the conflict are associated violent activities. Women experience the violence not only from the armed revivalists, but also from the armed personnel of the Indian Union. During counter insurgency operations, people are picked up by the army on suspicion. Besides *'disappearances'* and *disintegration of familial ties*, search operations conducted by the armed forces often result in *sexual violations* and *physical assaults*. Other than these two sources of violence, women are also subjected to a *spiraling level of violence on the domestic front*. Violence against women increases manifold under such circumstances.

> Writing on the conflict in Nagaland, Preeti Gill has observed. In the rural areas, continued violence has also resulted in *large-scale migration of young women to urban centres*. This leads to a number of problems as suddenly, the women find themselves cut off from their tribes, their village and their cultural moorings. Without any kind of effective support system, they become extremely vulnerable to violence and exploitation. It has been found that this has led to

> women being sexually exploited and even trafficked for work, or for sex. The incidence of *HIV/AIDS, drug abuse, alcohol and substance abuse* increases substantially in such a situation {Gill in Sen (Ed). 2006, pp. 218-219}.[20]

K. Ela of Prodigal Home, corroborates this view. Driven by poverty, unemployment and a weakened support system, many young women are lured into the flesh trade. These women are most vulnerable in getting infected by HIV/AIDS.

Relatively porous international borders have led to the effortless *trafficking of drugs* which has subsequently increased not only the incidence of drug abuse amongst the youth but also a vulnerability to HIV/AIDS, through the *sharing of infected needles*. According to a recent newspaper report, all Northeast Indian states bordering Myanmar are being subjected to the menace of drug abuse, consequential HIV infection and AIDS. The report stated, "Disclosed by the Health Minister of India, Anbumani Ramadoss recently, the pathetic tale describes Manipur and Nagaland as among the 'high HIV/AIDS prevalence' states, whereas Arunachal Pradesh and Mizoram are termed 'vulnerable' to the threat of HIV infection and AIDS"(www.narinjara.com/details.asp?id=1076).[21]

Elaborating on the repercussions of the prolonged armed conflict on women, Roshmi Goswami observed that, "continued violence in the rural areas has affected livelihoods, properties have been lost, there is lack of food security, lack of personal security even within one's own home and continued tension and stress. With many of the men getting killed or 'missing', there is an increase in the female-headed households" (Goswami, 2000, p.22).[22] Under such pressing situations, women have been burdened with additional socio-economic responsibilities. The heavy presence of the armed personnel as well as the armed revivalists moreover, *severely restrict the mobility of the women*, thereby limiting the work hours in the fields, which in turn infringe upon their food security.

Whether it be a direct consequence of the armed conflict or an indirect effect of drug abuse and AIDS, the fallouts are clearly evident. Broken homes, single mothers, unemployed and frustrated youth are all victims in the ensuing clashes between the competing interests.

Egypt

We have seen that the Arab Republic of Egypt has been witness to multiple changes in the political regimes, each professing its very own unique style of functioning. Changes in the political regimes, have also brought about transformations in the state policies and legal frameworks within which issues concerning women are looked at.

The United Nations International Conference on Population and Development (ICPD) held in Cairo in 1994 brought several of these issues to the fore and opened them up for public debate and discussion. Al-Ali has panted out the way pertinent fact that.

> The preparations as well as the conference itself created space for many women activists in Egypt to address previously taboo topics (abortion, violence, reproductive rights) or to discuss issues of common concern (equality before the law, political participation, structural adjustment, the Personal Status Law and nationality laws) with women from different political orientations and backgrounds (Al-Ali, 2002, p.11).[23]

Women's issues are often relegated to the vestiges of the prevalent dominant discourses. The matter is further complicated by the role of the Islamists and the relationship they share with the state authorities. Women's voices in these matters often go unheard and even if they are acknowledged, they are silenced or are unheeded.

Female Circumcision also called Female Genital Mutilation (FGM) is an issue that is in a midst of a raging debate. There are contradictory views from within the

Islamists—some vehemently condemn it as an un-Islamic practice while others support it. The matter was debated during the ICPD in 1994 and women's activists, regardless of their affiliations (Secular/Islamic), unanimously rejected the practice of female circumcision. The government, in an attempt to appease the international community, had proclaimed their commitment to enforce a legal ban on FGM. But after the conference was over, under the pressure of the conservative Al-Azhar, the government withdrew the ban on it.

As an advocacy based organization ECWR had organized an International Conference on FGM and Early Marriage from Religious and Legal perspectives on June 7-8, 2006 in Egypt, with its partners from 6 African countries and the U.K. to prepare a plan to fight FGM and Early Marriage (www.ecwronline.org).[24] 130 public figures including legal professionals, politicians and Islamic and Christian religious authorities, NGOs, journalists, and activists attended the conference from 21 countries. Several significant issues such as the relationship between poverty and FGM, role of the Parliament, the process of initiating and implementing legal amendments, role of economic empowerment in combating FGM, problems of the religious discourse and the way to influence it and mechanisms for eliminating FGM and challenges in the field, were discussed during the conference. The proceedings of the Conference came up with the following suggestions:

Mechanisms for eliminating FGM challenges in the field:

- Raising awareness on the dangers of FGM at the community level among both men and women rather than only among girls and their families.
- Training education and media professionals to disseminate knowledge as well as encouraging action from professionals, and Health, Population and Agricultural ministries.

- Introducing economic alternatives for circumcisers to help them refrain from it.
- Using real stories of girls highlighting success stories that could serve as a model to be followed.
- Involving youth in spreading awareness and organizing competitions for children and including illustrations, posters and brochures.
- Benefiting from communication technology and developing websites with books and resources on FGM and Early Marriage that speak out against these practices and their nature as social rather than religious traditions.

Legal mechanisms:

- Working to pass a law incriminating FGM (or amending the penal code in those countries with no law).
- Training lawyers, judges and police officers on how to use international agreements and regional courts and using international agreements in advocacy campaigns to lobby in parliaments about legislative amendments on FGM.
- Organizing parallel campaigns to address religious and cultural norms and taking part in regional conferences to exchange experiences and act together.
- Strengthening the role of civil society organizations in pursuing and reporting FGM practitioners.
- Launching an international campaign to stop FGM and urging governments to take decisive positions.
- Taking action on international agreements and lobbying non-member states to ratify them.

Religious discourse and how to influence it:

- Advocating for a statement signed by religious leaders

and public figures and distributing it locally and regionally.

- Promoting partnership between official and religious institutions and civil society; and supporting the role of civil society organizations in enforcing the state's strategies to stopping FGM.
- Providing religious leaders with medical information on FGM's risks and convince them to "do no harm."
- Making best use of advocacy mechanisms to stop FGM with an emphasis on the advocacy in the media and audiovisual media unifying the religious discourse.
- Strengthening dialogue between religious leaders and increase dialogue with members of parliament and relevant official institutions.
- Encouraging veteran scientists to write more about FGM.
- Distributing printed material in mosques and churches.

It was believed that if, not all, but even a few of these measures could be implemented, a lot could be achieved in this field.

Other issues of reproductive health, which are of utmost concern to women in Egypt, are *birth control and abortion*. According to Azza M. Karam.

> On the one hand, the Egyptian government is in favour of family planning to reduce the so called 'population explosion'. Contraception, in the form of the pill and the coil, are encouraged, and the pill in fact is supplied at heavily subsidized prices and is almost free. Family planning clinics are readily available, and the advertisements about the necessity to reduce the size of the family have become part and parcel of local popular discourse. On the other hand, what is openly problematic for some women's groups, in relation to reproductive rights, is the issue of abortion, which is a

> very tricky one. Government policy is supposedly based on religious interpretations and indicates that pregnant women are allowed a legal abortion only if their health is threatened. Abortion in this event can take place within the first three months of pregnancy (Karam, 1998,pp. 171-172).[25]

Another subject of much interest to women is Veiling. Sa'ad Zaghloul was the first proponent of lifting the veil for Egyptian women. After his return from exile, he entered the tents of the women welcomers and met Hoda Sharawi wearing a hijab. He extended his hand, removed her veil from her face and he laughed (www.ecwronline.org/english/researches/index.htm).[26] Several decades after this historical moment, the debate on veiling has re-emerged in the socio-political landscape of Egypt.

More and more women, today in Egypt are donning the veil. This phenomenon raises important questions regarding the increasing wave of conservatism in the Egyptian society as well as the shifts taking place in the social patterns of the community. In the scheme of daily life of women in Egypt, the *Hijab* has acquired a symbolic value of modesty, virtue and traditional mores. It is no longer just an attire but also a way of life for many.

Sherifa Zuhur conducted a study on Cairene women in the fall of 1988, with the objective of finding out whether women could explain the prevailing dominant image conveyed to them, how satisfactorily it performed, how they interpreted the Islamists' code of behaviour for women, and whether they felt that the Islamist image of womanhood was moving to usurp the dominant image's position (Zuhur, 1992, pp.58-59).[27] She surveyed fifty women, of which 62 percent were veiled (*muhaggabat*). They wore the modern version of the *hijab* and the *khimar,* and within this category also various costume interpretations existed. There were other women who wore a headscarf that covered the throat or was draped around the shoulders, but wore western clothing beneath. Others labeled these women as partial *muhaggabat* or fad followers. 14 percent of the women surveyed were *munaqqabat,* that is they completely covered their faces with a face veil (niqab) and often wore gloves as well as the hijab. The remaining 38 percent of the women surveyed were unveiled.

The study revealed a few very interesting insights into the changing world of Egyptian women. Sherifa Zuhur observed that, the majority of the younger veiled women saw the *hijab* as a symbol of change. This change was not only a personal and moral decision, but represented a social sisterhood to them. These veiled women under thirty had been wearing a *hijab* on the average for seven years. The *munaqqabat* had been wearing the veil for an average of four years after 'graduating' from the ordinary *hijab* (Zuhur, 1992, p.76).[28]

She also stated how several respondents described their decision to don their veil as a momentous one, made after a period of introspection. In her study, unveiled women had reported that the *hijab* had caught the fancy of the university students and working- women because they were paid to do so by the *Ikhwan* and other groups. But there was no evidence to authenticate this suggestion.

Another study done by Yvonne Haddad in 1984 on the reasons why women took to veiling in Egypt, Jordan, Oman, Kuwait, and the United States revealed a variety of explanations (cited in Zuhur, 1992, p.104).[29] They can be listed as follows:

- Religious: An act of obedience to the will of God as a consequence of a profound religious experience, which several women referred to as being "born again".
- Psychological: An affirmation of authenticity, a return to the roots, and a rejection of Western norms (One woman talked about the "end of turmoil" and a "sense of peace").

- Political: A sign of disenchantment with the prevailing political order.
- Revolutionary: An identification with the Islamic revolutionary forces that affirm the necessity of the Islamization of the society as the only means of salvation.
- Economic: A sign of affluence, of being a lady of leisure.
- Cultural: A public affirmation of allegiance to chastity and modesty, of not being a sex object (especially among unmarried working women).
- Demographic: A sign of being urbanized.
- Practical: A means of reducing the amount to be spent on clothing. Some respondents claimed that others were receiving money from Libya and Saudi Arabia for the purpose.
- Domestic: A way to keep the peace, since the males in the family insist on it.

Commenting on this study, Zuhur stated–

> Her assessments accorded with my data, although the "economic" category of explanation is problematic. The veiled respondents simply did not offer that sort of explanation for their orientation, and they clearly were not ladies of leisure. My respondents offered explanations for their veiling included in the "cultural", "religious" and "psychological" categories. The wearing of hijab to women identifying with an Islamic ideal is a "new" badge of authenticity (Zuhur, 1992, p.105).[30]

The two studies thus reveal that the choice to don the veil is not merely borne out of a strengthened religious conviction but is also shaped by a myriad of social and economic forces playing in the society.

Another pertinent issue that concerns women is the *right to work*. Although legal provisions have been provided to safeguard the right of women to work in Egypt, the reality falls far short of the expectations the Civil Servants System, promulgated by Law No. 47/1978, and the Public Sector Employees System, promulgated by Law No. 48/1978, were enacted in order to apply the principle of women's right to work. Both laws contain provisions to help women (and their spouses) working in the government and public sector to reconcile their duties to their families with their responsibilities to their place of employment in accordance with article 11 of the Constitution (Karam, 1998, pp.158-159).[31]

Despite wide ranging benefits provided for the women within the legal framework, gaps remain. While certain fields of work such as the judiciary are still out of bounds for women, in certain other areas like defence, their representation is merely symbolic.

Other than the lapses in the implementation of the labour laws in their true sense, the views held by certain sections of the clergy as well as the lay public, have fuelled the debate revolving around women's right to work. Very often officials in the government as well as the clergy contend that the only way to solve the rising problem of unemployment facing the country would be to persuade women to leave their jobs for men and return to their domestic duties! By extolling the virtues of woman as a mother and someone whose religious duty it is to nurture her children for the growth and development of the country, attempts are being made to discourage women from working and deprive them of their right to employment.

Thus we see how issues pertaining to the basic rights of women—whether it is health, employment or simply a 'right to be oneself', gets enmeshed in the entangled discontents in the society. In the battle between the revivalists and the state authorities, the women have to bear the brunt. In this chaotic maze, the voices of the women are often muted and lost. Concerted efforts by the women as well as the powers that be need to be adopted to retrieve these voices and further their cause ahead.

REFERENCES

1 http://www.ecwronline.org/english/researches/index.htm Accessed on 14/11/06

2 Interview with Ms. K. Ela, Director, Prodigal Home, on 2 February 2007, Dimapur, Nagaland.

3 Interview with Ms. Nehad A. Komsan, ECWR, on 26 November 2006, Cairo, Egypt.

4 *Ibid.*

5 *Ibid.*

6 Interview with Pastor Dirang Lungalang, 1st February 2007, Chumukedima, Nagaland.

7 Interview with Ms. K. Ela, Director, Prodigal Home, on 2 February 2007, Dimapur, Nagaland

8 *Ibid.*

9 Interview with Ms. Nehad A. Komsan, ECWR, on 26 November 2006, Cairo, Egypt

10 *Ibid.*

11 Al-Ali, N.S. (2002). *The Women's Movement in Egypt with selected references to Turkey. Civil Society and Social Movements Programme*, Paper No.5. United Nations Research Institute of Social Development.

12 *Ibid.*

13 Interview with Ms. Nehad A. Komsan, ECWR, on 26 November 2006, Cairo, Egypt

14 *Ibid.*

15 *Ibid.*

16 Ruivah, K (1993). Social Changes Among The Nagas (Tangkhul) in Goswami, T (2006). *Role of Women as Peace Builders with Special Reference to Nagaland.* Guwahati: Peace Studies, Omeo Kumar Das Institute of Social Change & Development.

17 Interview with Ms. K. Ela, Director, Prodigal Home, on 2 February 2007, Dimapur, Nagaland

18 *Ibid.*

19 Goswami, R (2000). *Documentation of Human Rights Violations of Women in the State of Assam in North East India: A Report.* North East Network, Shillong, India.

20 Gill, P (2006) Women in Time of Conflict: The case of Nagaland in Sen, G (Ed), *Where the Sun Rises When Shadows Fall: The North East.* New Delhi: Oxford University Press.

21 http://www.narinjara.com/details.asp?id=1076 Accessed on 13th February 2007.

22 Goswami, R. (2000). *Documentation of Human Rights Violations of Women in the State of Assam in North East India: A Report.* North East Network, Shillong, India.

23 Al-Ali, N.S. (2002). *The Women's Movement in Egypt with selected references to Turkey. Civil Society and Social Movements Programme*, Paper No. 5. United Nations Research Institute of Social Development.

24 www.ecwronline.org Accessed on 14 November 2006

25 Karam, A.M. (1998). *Women, Islamisms and the State: Contemporary Feminisms in Egypt.* Great Britain: Macmillan Press & United States of America: St. Martin's Press, Inc.

26 Komsan, N.A. and Borai, N.Al (2003). *Liberation of the Arab Woman: From Coast to Coast.* Paper presented at the Arab Women's Forum, Cairo. In http://www.ecwronline.org/english/researches/index.htm

Accessed on 15 November 2006.

27 Zuhur, S. (1992). Revealing Reveiling: Islamist Gender Ideology *In Contemporary Egypt.* Albany: State University of New York Press.

28 *Ibid.*

29 *Ibid.*

30 *Ibid.*

31 Karam, A.M. (1998). *Women, Islamisms and the State: Contemporary Feminisms in Egypt.* Great Britain: Macmillan Press & United States of America: St. Martin's Press, Inc.

VI

CONCLUSION

The preceding chapters have clearly carved out the dynamics within which women initiate efforts of conflict transformation. The contexts of conflict in Nagaland and Egypt are no doubt in contrast to each other, yet they both comprise certain similar elements that provide a virginal ground for women's activism.

The dynamics shared between the state authorities and the revivalists in the two contexts, have created a milieu within which women have had to bear the brunt of the widespread repercussions. Caught in the vortex, are their basic rights and concerns. Conflict transformation is a long and a relatively slow process and it aims not only at developing capacity but also supporting structural changes within the context of conflict.

Women, who have taken it upon themselves to initiate efforts of bringing about changes within the conflict scenario, have had to face a gargantuan task ahead. Not only are they facing stiff resistance from the state authorities but also equally strong opposition from the revivalists. The nature of resistance may not be directly confrontational but even subtle forces of antagonism can dissuade such efforts.

The notions of gender and nation are intricately intertwined. Women are often acknowledged as the cultural symbols of a nation and are burdened with carrying forward the legacy. As such, in times of conflict, the women are the first to be targeted...not only as victims of the violent ramifications but also utilized as shelter providers of the oppressors. As to Negowetti, observes,

> Women participate in ethnic and national processes as biological reproducers of an ethnic collectivity, as reproducers of the nation's boundaries, as key participants in the ideological reproduction of the collectivity and as transmitters of its culture, as signifiers of national differences and as participants in the national, political and economic struggles (www.skynet.ie/~peacesoc/read nationmasculinity.html).[1]

As has been reflected in the present study, revivalists in both Nagaland and Egypt have issued diktats on the dress code of women. In their attempt to save their cultures from so called moral corruption and social degradation, the creation of a 'virtuous woman', dressed more conservatively in traditional attire, is an image strongly espoused by the revivalists.

The attire of the woman becomes a symbol of the cultural purity of a people. Islamic revivalists encourage women to wear the veil, and therefore in Egypt, today, a lot more women have begun to don the veil, either in the form of a headscarf or the *hijab*. In Nagaland, the ethnic revivalists had issued a dress code for women a few years ago, although due to massive public opposition, it could not see the light of day. Yet in other conflict prone areas in the North Eastern region of India, such as the Bodo Territorial Autonomous District Council (in Assam) and in Manipur, ethnic revivalists have issued similar diktats and have been successful in realizing them!

Another aspect common to both these contexts is the dismal political participation of women. Since attaining the statehood in 1965, Nagaland has seen a few excellent women parliamentarians, yet the numbers are far below expectations. In Egypt on the other hand, women constitute a mere 18% of the diplomats, that is, 161 out of a total of 900 (www.sis.gov.eg/En/Pub/magazin/summer/2002/110223000000000008.htm).[2] Although, the presence of women in localized informal settings is highly visible, their relative absence from formal sites of power, prevent the proper redressal of grievances. This ultimately creates gaps in the process of highlighting issues that concern women, at the policy level.

Despite all odds, women in both Nagaland and Egypt have organized themselves into collectives to work towards upholding the rights of women. Utilizing their professional skills to the best possible level, the women have initiated steps to overcome the hindrances and promote an understanding in their respective communities about the significance of women-related issues.

Continuous and sustained effort is the key to bringing about changes within the conflict scenario and it is efforts like these that will ultimately usher in the process of social transformation.

REFERENCES

1 http://www.skynet.ie/~peacesoc/read/nationmasculinity.html Accessed on 14 September 2006.

2 http:// www.sis.gov.eg/En/Pub/magazin/summer/2002/110223000000000008.htm Accessed on 10 September 2006.

BIBLIOGRAPHY

Austin, A, Fischer, M & Ropers, N (Eds.) *Transforming Ethnopolitical Conflict: The Berghof Handbook*. Germany: VS Verlag Fur Sozialwissenschaften.

Badran, M. (1996). *Feminists, Islam and Nation: Gender and the Making of Modern Egypt*. Egypt: American University in Cairo Press.

Cousens, E.M., Kumar, C &Wermester, K (Eds.) *Peacebuilding as Politics: Cultivating Peace in Fragile Societies*. USA & UK: Lynne Rienner Publishers, Inc.

Esposito, John L and John O Voll (1996). *Islam and Democracy*. New York and Oxford: Oxford University Press.

Esposito, John L. (1998). *Islam: The Straight Path* (Third Edition). Oxford University Press: New York and Oxford.

Esposito, John L (Ed.). (1997). *Political Islam: Revolution, Radicalism or Reform*. Egypt: The American University in Cairo Press.

Goswami, T (2006). *Role of Women as Peace Builders with Special Reference to Nagaland*. India: Peace Studies, Omeo Kumar Das Institute of Social Change and Development (OKDISCD), Guwahati, Assam.

Kabeer, Naila (1994). *Reversed Realities: Gender Hierarchies in Development Thought*. New York and London: Verso.

Karam, Azza M (1998). *Women, Islamisms and the State: Contemporary Feminisms in Egypt*. Great Britain: Macmillan Press and U.S.A: St. Martin's Press, Inc.

Khashim, R (1993). *Social Changes Among The Nagas (Tangkhul)*. New Delhi: Cosmo Publications.

Lasuh, W. & Nuh, V K (2002). *The Naga Chronicle*. New Delhi: Regency.

Mark, R (1996). *Research Made Simple: A Handbook for Social Workers*. London, Delhi & USA: Sage Publications.

Miall, H, Ramsbotham, O and Woodhouse, T (1999). *Contemporary Conflict Resolution*. UK: Polity Press and USA: Blackwell Publishers.

Moser, C O N & Clark, F C (2001). *Victims, Perpetrators or Actors? Gender, Armed Conflict and Political Violence*. New Delhi: Kali for Women.

Sen, G (Ed) (2006), *Where the Sun Rises When Shadows Fall: The North East*. New Delhi: Oxford University Press

Sherman, E & Reid, W.J. (Eds). (1994). *Qualitative Research in Social Work*. New York: Columbia University Press.

Skjelsbaek, I & Smith, D (Eds.).(2001). *Gender, Peace and Conflict*. London, California and New Delhi: Sage Publications.

Smith, J A, Rom Harrę' and K V Lagenhove (Eds.).(1995). *Rethinking Methods in Psychology*. London: Sage Publications.

Syed, Mohammad Ali (2004). *The Position of Women in Islam: A Progressive View*. Albany: State University of New York Press.

Wimmer, A, Goldstone, R J, Horowitz, D, Joras, U & Schetter, C (2004). *Facing Ethnic Conflicts: Toward a New Realism*. USA: Rowman & Littlefield Publishers, Inc.

Wolff, S &Schneckener, U (Ed.) *Managing and Settling Ethnic Conflicts: Perspectives on Successes and Failures in Europe, Africa and Asia*. UK: C. Hurst & Co. Ltd.

Yuval-Davis, Nira (1997). *Gender and Nation*. London, California and New Delhi: Sage Publications.

Zuhur, S (1992). *Revealing Reveiling: Islamist Gender Ideology in Contemporary Egypt*. Albany: State University of New York Press.

Articles

Al-Ali, Nadje S. *The Women's Movement in Egypt with Selected References to Turkey*, Civil Society and Social Movements Programme, Paper No. 5, April 2002, United Nations Research Institute For Social Development (UNRISD).

Anderlini, S N (2003) *Causes of Conflict: A Brief Overview* (Power Point Presentation for UNIFEM). Women Waging Peace.

Gahramanova, A (2006). *Identity Conflicts and Its Implications For Conflict Management*. UNISCI Discussion Papers, No.11.

Komsan, N A and Borai, N Al (2003). *Liberation of the Arab Woman: From Coast to Coast*. Paper presented at the Arab Women's Forum, Cairo. In http://www.ecwronline.org/english/researches/index.htm (Accessed on 15 November 2006).

Murshid, Tazeen Mahnaz *Women, Islam And the State: Subordination and Resistance*, University of London, In http://www.lib.uchicago.edu/e/su/southasia/Tazeen.html

Nigowetti, Nicole. *Nationalism and Gender: The Construction of Identity* In_http://www.skynet.ie/~peacesoc/read/nationmasculinity.html Accessed on 14 September 2006.

Rothchild, Donald and David A. Lake. *Ethnic Fears and Global Engagement of Ethnic Conflict: The International Spread and Management,* Institute on Global Conflict and Cooperation, IGCC Policy Papers, University of California Multi-Campus Research Unit, 1996.

Journals

Dutta, A (2002). Women in Conflict Situation: A Case Study of Assam. *Journal of Social Change & Development*, Vol. 1, No.1. Guwahati: Omeo Kumar Das Institute of Social Change and Development.

Mc Loughlin (Jr.), W.G. (1959). *Modern Revivalism: Charles Grandison Finney to Billy Graham.* American Sociological Review, Volume 24,No.5. New York: Ronald Press Co.

Ong, Aihwa State versus Islam: Malay Families, Women's Bodies, and the Body Politic in Malaysia, *American Ethnologist*, Vol. 17, No. 2 (May), pp. 258-276,1990.

Reports

Goswami, R (2000). Documentation of Human Rights Violations of Women in the State of Assam in North East India: *A Report*. North East Network, Shillong, India.

Websites

http://mediaguidetoislam.sfsu.edu/03a_feminism.htm Accessed on 3 September 2006

http://www.indiatogether.org/2005/nov/pce-nagaland.htm Accessed on 10 September 2006

http://www.sis.gov.eg/En/Pub/magazin/summer2002/102230000000000008.htm Accessed on 13 September 2006.

http://www.safraproject.org/sgi-intro.htm#Sexuality Accessed on 13 September 2006

http://www.skynet.ie/~peacesoc/read/nationmasculinity.html Accessed on 14 September 2006

www.wikipedia.org Accessed on 14 September 2006.

http://en.wikipedia.org/wiki/Heinz-Kohut Accessed on 22 September 2006 http://www.colorado.edu/conflict/peace/problem/denyid.htm Accessed on 22 September 2006

http://www.psych.neu.edu/ISSI/daily.htm Accessed on 22 September 2006

http://www.beyondintractability.org/essay/social_psychological Accessed on 25 September 2006

http://www.beyondintractability.org/action/essay.jsp?id=36017&nid=192 Accessed on 25 September 2006

http://www.psych.neu.edu/ISSI/daily.htm Accessed on 30 September 2006

http://www.colorado.edu/conflict/transform/northrup.htm Accessed on 3 October 2006

http://iadc.iwa.org/en/Unit1.htm Accessed on 12 October 2006

www.globalsecurity.org/military/library/policy/army/fm/100-20/10020gl.htm Accessed on 15 October 2006

http://www.thefreedictionary.com/revivalism Accessed on 22 October 2006

http://columbia.thefreedictionary.com/Islam+(concept) Accessed on 22 October 2006

http://www.jstor.org/view/00405841/ap050108/05a00050/0 Accessed on 22 October 2006

http://www.un.org/womenwatch/osagi/pdf/res1325.pdf Accessed on 27 October 2006

http://www.igw.org/peace/peacebuilding/raising-womens-voices.html Accessed on 27 October 2006

http://www.trinstitute.org/ojpcr/3_3rev.htm Accessed on 27 October 2006

http://meria.idc.ac.il/journal/2001/issue1/jv5n1a6.html Accessed on 29 October 2006 http://www.manipuronline.com/Features/August2002/nagawomenunion23_1.htm Accessed on 31 October 2006

http://en.wikipedia.org/wiki/Qualitative_research Accessed on 3 November 2006

http://www.nova.edu/ssss/QR/BackIssues/QR2-1/aronson.html Accessed on 9 November 2006

http://en.wikipedia.org/wiki/Interview Accessed on 9 November 2006

http://en.wikipedia.org/wiki/Structured_interview Accessed on 13 November 2006

http://pandc.ca/?cat=carl_rogers&page=rogerian_theory Accessed on 14 November 2006

http://www.ecwronline.org/english/researches/index.htm Accessed on 14 November 2006

http://allpsych.com/psychology101/defenses.html Accessed on 15 November 2006.

http://www.haverford.edu/psych/ddavis/p.109g/erikson.stages.html Accessed on 20 November 2006

Interviews

Interview with Ms. Nehad A. Komsan, Director, ECWR, on 26 November 2006, Cairo, Egypt.

Interview with Pastor Dirang Lungalang, 1 February 2007, Chumukedima, Nagaland.

Interview with Ms. K Ela, Director, Prodigal Home, on 2 February 2007, Dimapur, Nagaland.

APPENDICES

QUESTIONNAIRE FOR EGYPT

The researcher assures that confidentiality shall be maintained:

- Gender: Male / Female
- Age:
- Marital Status:
  - a. Single
  - b. Widow
  - c. Married
  - d. Separated
- Level of Education:
  - a. Illiterate
  - b. Below Secondary Degree
  - c. Secondary Degree.
  - d. University Degree.
  - e. Post Univ. Degree.
- Can you tell me a bit about the History of the organization:
  - a. Name of the organization.
  - b. When was it established?
  - c. Why was it established?
  - d. What are its objectives?
  - e. What are its projects and programmes for women?
- Can you tell me how you locate the historical legacy of the women's movement in Egypt? Can you tell me a little about the origin of the women's movement?

- How different is the Feminist movement from the Women's rights movement? Is there a point of intersection for both? Do they have common issues to contend with?
- How do the women locate themselves between the State and the conservatives?
- Do you think, the State policies are in line with those of the women's activists?
- What kind of issues are the women' activists /the woman's organization struggling for? (Equal rights for the women/ Political Empowerment/ better rights for women within the Sharia Law etc)?
- How are the struggles over these issues located within Islam and between the Moderates and the Conservatives?
- What strategies have been adopted to counter the growing Revivalism? Or what are the organizational policies towards it? Is it perceived as a problem in the first place?
- Do you have to tailor your organization's programmes for women, keeping in mind the prevalent 'restrictions'? (Restrictions referring to the limited mobility of women, taboo related to the discussion of issues such as birth control, FGM, and political/social/economic empowerment).
- Have there been any obstacles faced by the organization in its interactions with the revivalists/traditionalists regarding the projects and programmes?
- As a woman's organization...or an organization working for women, how do you view the changing face of women in Egypt today (taking into account both the move towards globalization as well as the rise of conservatism amongst women)?
- Do you think women's spaces have become more gendered? Do you think the new trend has restricted women's mobility and proved an obstacle for her growth?

- How do you envisage the future of women's activism in the years to come? And what issues do you think need to be focused on more seriously?

QUESTIONNAIRE FOR NAGALAND

The researcher assures that confidentiality shall be maintained:

- Gender: Male / Female
- Age:
- Marital Status:
  - a. Single
  - b. Widow
  - c. Married
  - d. Separated
- Level of Education:
  - a. Illiterate
  - b. Below Secondary Degree
  - c. Secondary Degree.
  - d. University Degree.
  - e. Post Univ. Degree.
- Can you tell me a bit about the History of the organization:
  - a. Name of the organization.
  - b. When was it established?
  - c. Why was it established?
  - d. What are its objectives?
  - e. What are its projects and programmes for women?
- Can you tell me how you locate the historical legacy of the

women's movement in Nagaland? Can you tell me a little about the origin of the women's movement?

- How different is the Feminist movement from the Women's rights movement? Is there a point of intersection for both? Do they have common issues to contend with?
- How do the women locate themselves between the State and the insurgents?
- Do you think, the State policies are in line with those of the women's activists?
- What kind of issues are the women' activists /the woman's organization struggling for? (Equal rights for the women/ Political Empowerment/ better rights for women / Inheritance rights)?
- How are the struggles over these issues located between the State and the Insurgent organizations?
- What strategies have been adopted to counter the growing Insurgency (ethnic revivalism)? Or what are the organizational policies towards it? Is it perceived as a problem in the first place?
- Have the growing struggles for a separate ethnic identity have any impact on the position and status of women in the society and home? Has it affected the women in terms of their restricted mobility, dressing more conservatively etc.? (Has a diktat ever been issued by the various groups making it compulsory for women to wear the traditional dress of *mekhela*...like their counterparts in Bodoland).
- Do you have to tailor your organization's programmes for women, keeping in mind the prevalent 'restrictions'? (Restrictions referring to the limited mobility of women, taboo related to the discussion of issues such as birth control (role of the Church), and political/social/economic empowerment).

- Have there been any obstacles faced by the organization in its interactions with the revivalists/traditionalists regarding the projects and programmes?
- As a woman's organization...or an organization working for women, how do you view the changing face of women in Nagaland today?
- Do you think women's spaces have become more gendered? Do you think the new trend has restricted women's mobility and proved an obstacle for her growth?
- How do you envisage the future of women's activism in the years to come? And what issues do you think need to be focused on more seriously?

2. Transcripts of Interviews

2.1 Transcript of Interview with Ms. Nehad Abul Komsan (26 Novemver 2006)

Name	:	Nehad Abul Komsan
Age	:	35 years
Marital Status	:	Married
Education	:	Post University Degree
Profession	:	Lawyer/ Social Worker.
Name of Organization	:	Egyptian Centre for Women's Rights (ECWR)
Designation	:	Director.
Year of Establishment	:	1998

* Origin and need to establish ECWR:

"After the International Conference on Population and Development held in Cairo in 1994, legislations for women were reviewed for the first time. The conference brought a lot of issues to the forefront and several significant issues were discussed on a public platform. The review of the available legislations also revealed the discriminatory policies towards women. There has been an absence of a woman's movement since the 1950s. The 1960s and 70s onwards saw the emergence of several noted women's activists but no organized women's movement." The ICPD in 1994 provided an impetus for an organization to champion the legal rights of women and thus ECWR was born (my paraphrasing).

"At that time, we realized the need for an organization that could provide legal assistance to the women. We use direct assistance as an instrument to understand the legislation better. It is a practical approach and we focus on the grassroots. They teach us more than we teach them." (referring to working with women at the grassroots).

Kind of Organization

"ECWR is basically an advocacy-based organization. It is not a charitable or a service-oriented organization. It is a centre promoting the legal and political rights of women. Its aim is to assist women to get empowered. The absence of women in high levels of decision-making, made us realize the need to groom women in leadership skills and the dire need for the political empowerment of women. The main thrust of ECWR is human rights: to raise women's awareness as human rights."

Issues dealt with

"When we first established ECWR in 1996, we decided to focus on women who were not registered at birth. We decided to take one village as a case study and reveal to the people what it entailed to be without *birth certificates*. Having no birth certificates meant being out of record. Being out of the official records meant being deprived of state policies and benefits like pensions, subsidies for medical treatment, education, jobs and the entire gamut of developmental programmes."

"Initially no one perceived this as a problem but we took it upon ourselves to convey to the various governmental departments in a language they could understand. To try and make people understand the magnitude of the problem, we tried to interpret it in a manner they could understand better. So we told the politicians and the political parties that they were missing out on a vote bank and as rightful citizens of the country, these people should be given electoral cards to exercise their right to vote. To the Ministry of Interior, we told them that people who were out of the records could pose to be a security scare and could be bad for the overall security of the nation. To the Ministry of Health, it was told that unless they knew about the total population of a place, they could not effectively implement their policies and programs and would more often than not, face the ire of the people for their ineffectiveness. Thus the attempt of creating a language that people understood went a long way in helping the people take this problem seriously and acknowledge it as a reality in the current context."

"With regards to the issue of *Female Genital Mutilation (FGM)* and the issue of *Early Marriages*, we try to take it up from a legal standpoint and try to relate to it from the people's point of view. Our experience has shown that when we discuss it with villagers, they say that they practice FGM because they want to protect their daughters. They also believe that getting their daughters married off early could ensure a good life for them. So ECWR decided to work for the education of the girls. In Egypt, till 18 years of age, education is free and in primary school the annual fee is about 8 dollars. So we took the matter up with the Ministry of Education to see if this annual fee can be reduced."

Problems from the Islamists

"We are not facing any problem from *fundamentalists*. From Islamists, we face lots of funny issues. We use religious language to prove our point. We use traditions, because we know all traditions are not good and all are not bad. We work with both mosques and churches."

Problems from the State

"The main problem we face is in terms of *State Security*. It is easy to work on people's stomach. But once you ignite people's minds, then it could create problems for the state. They cancelled ECWR's Women's Day Celebration because they heard that around 1000 women were supposed to come. Censorship through State Security is basically in the form of:

- Canceling activities.
- Not approving funds for projects.
- Terrorizing staff.

Igniting minds to question the policies and advocate for better education, health, electricity etc. can be frightening for the state authorities. The Government prefers to keep people ignorant, as they are scared that more informative as well as politically aware people can oust them from power. When we worked with the villagers, we tried to help them question the role of the Local Council. Many of them didn't even know what the Local Council or an election was. We had to ask them, when was the last time your wall was dirtied by sticking pictures or bills...that was the local council elections. An ironical incident but it also reveals the extent of ignorance of the people at the grassroots, who are not only deprived of their rightful status but also excluded from the participatory political process."

Rise in Conservatism in Egypt

"The reason for the rise in conservatism in Egypt today is mainly political. Egypt was under British occupation. In 1952, the people's revolution took place. Before the Revolution, politically, Egypt was very liberal. During the 50s and the 60s, the Communist forces came to power. The Communist party was against the multi-party system. When Nasser came to power, Egypt began to look up...politically and socially. Egypt won the war with Israel. There was industrialization and things were looking up. People felt that had money. Women were elected as Ministers and Ambassadors under his regime. Therefore people felt victorious. When Sadat came to power, people couldn't acknowledge him as their leader and for long accepted him as Nasser's shadow."

"Just after the Revolution, about 4 million Egyptians went to Saudi Arabia for work. When they came back, they returned not only with more monetary wealth accrued from the oil industry but also conservative ideas regarding Islam. This was because, the most conservative school of thought in Islam, the *Wahabi ideology,* has its origins in Saudi Arabia. Anwar Sadat, tried to win over the political Islamists to his side and thus, chose to forge an alliance with the Muslim Brotherhood. During those years, there were several attempts by the Brotherhood to impose through religious ideology their views on FGM and early marriages. Now, nearly 30 years after it all begun, it has begun bearing fruits. Conservatism has increased manifold and has become a visible force in the Egyptian society. The *Wahabi ideology* has made Islam a 'cosmetic rather than a value issue'. When you mix religion and politics, you tend to destroy both."

"The Egyptian culture actually is very peaceful and very tolerant. The influence of the Coptic tradition can also be seen in many of our traditional practices, especially in agriculture. Al Azhar, which is regarded in high esteem by the Sunni community, is increasingly coming under the influence of the finances of Saudi Arabia, thus implying that the clout of the *Wahabi* school is increasing, thus making it a haven for ultra-conservatives."

*Whether there is an *intersection between Women's Rights and Feminist movement:*

"The issues are not clearly defined in both and they tend to often overlap. For nearly fifty years now, there have been a number of women's activists, but no women's movement per se. Besides the term 'women's movement' is a broad term and connotes several things at once."

Politicization of Issues

" The issue of the *Hijab* is more a political issue rather than a social issue. The current controversies regarding it are a result of the interaction between contradictory political forces, such as,

a) Nasserist vs. Sadatist ideology.

b) Egypt vs. Saudi Arabia.

Similarly, the issue of Early Marriage is a result of the interaction between economic and political factors i.e., the debate between Poverty and Lack of Education. Also controversies such as the one regarding maternity leave should be looked at from a wider perspective." The matter cannot be merely termed a "woman's issue" and swept under the carpet. The demand for a leave during the fragile months, does not justify a demand for regular vacation...there is no holidaying ....it is hard work, and women have every right to demand for it! (My paraphrasing)

What are the obstacles faced by the organization in working for women's rights and championing the cause of women's empowerment (social/legal/political/economic)?

"The problems are as follows:

a) We have a dictatorship regime and women's issues are not the foremost on the list of priority issues. If at all, it is the least.

b) There is an unhealthy, hidden coalition between political Islamists and the Government. It is what I call the Heaven-Devil alliance. Political Islamists through their religious efforts try to make people invisible from the political landscape and not question the government. The Government is fully aware of this and allows it to happen. They allow the Political Islamists to metaphorically speaking, 'drug the people to sleep' but they also have the ultimate say, in that they prevent them (i.e. the Political Islamists) from emerging as the all powerful...and exercise restraint when necessary.

c) Our rich, tolerant traditional culture has become increasingly polluted by the Azhar traditions. In fact, through their efforts they are trying to make bad traditions, a holy issue.

d) The prevalent economic situation.

e) The awful law controlling the NGOs in the country.

f) We have NGOs and activists but no organized, joint movement per se. The CEDAW Shadow report was a successful effort by different NGOs and activists, but the same cannot be said about the Beijing+5 Platform.

g) The shortage of funds from the Government for the NGOs is a big obstacle. For any funds to come in, there needs to be an approval from the State security and this makes the circle quite tight."

Main Aim of the Movement for Women's Rights

"The aim of the movement should be the Capacity Building of the NGOs and the activists. Once that is achieved and the fear from the state security is broken down, a lot more can get done. Technical expertise is no doubt required, but more important than that is to empower the people and make strategic plans for the future."

"Building self-confidence of the women is the first step. It is important to *help her build vision*. ECWR has Small Initiative Programmes for women. A fixed amount of money is given as an endowment to a woman who comes with an idea to market it. The money is given in installments and it is not demanded back by ECWR. The programme is solely dependent on the original ideas of the women and their acumen to market the product. I feel that programmes must be context specific...the same programme need not be successful everywhere. For example, I personally feel that the *Grameen Bank* concept should not have been replicated everywhere, it led to the destruction of moral values creating violence and hatred. I believe that the ideas should come from the women themselves as they know their communities best."

2.2 Transcript of Interview with Ms. ELA (Interview on 2 February, 207)

Name : K. Ela

Age : 35 Years.

Sex Female.

Education : Masters of Arts

Profession : Social Worker

Marital Status : Single

Name of Organization : Prodigals' Home.

Designation : Director

Year of Establishment : 1990

Why was it Established?

In the late 1980's and 1990's, the incidence of drug addiction had increased manifold in the state. *Prodigals' Home* was established by the founder director to address this problem. Over the years, it expanded its area of operation to include

Injected Drug Users (IDU) and male drug users. Today, it also works with male and female drug users, sex workers, street and slum children etc. The organization also runs a Short Stay Home for women and girls who need a place to stay. The inmates are sent to other centres for vocational training while skills like basket weaving and needlework are taught in the organization itself. Once trained, the women are incorporated within the organization. The organization also focuses on female school dropouts.

Projects and Programmes for Women

The organization tries to address problems concerning women in rural areas...such as encouraging the habit of saving and formation of SHGs. To improve the economic condition of the women, training on organic kitchen garden and community gardens are encouraged. Through shared labour, they could earn profits.

Programmes of Rural Development directed towards general people...provide awareness regarding how to access schemes from the Government, promote indigenous art and craft and help people market their products. We organize Regional level fairs. We also help the artisans opt for the Life Insurance policy as developed by the Government for them.

In the rural areas, our focus is mainly on Developmental programmes. While in the urban areas, the focus is mainly on HIV/AIDS and drug abuse prevention. We also have Drop-in Centres where patients can come and stay the whole day as well as be imparted information on HIV/AIDS.

Women's Movement in Nagaland

I cannot say that there is a movement per se. Although there have been improvements in the scenario over the ages. Initially, the State Women's Commission came into existence. The Naga Mothers Association too began on a high note, but as of now, it is rather stagnant.

** To the question if the NMA shares any relation with any Under Ground Women's organization such as NSWON (National Socialist Women of Nagalim).

The bond is always there between women, whether underground or over-ground. The bond will remain forever.

I personally don't agree with talks of women equaling the status of men. The gaps remain because we have not really looked into issues through the Rights perspective.

How do the women locate themselves between the state and the insurgents?

Definitely, the conflict situation has worsened the scenario (drug abuse/sex work not just among women but also men). Even in the case of drug abuse, one way or other, the inflow of drugs has increased. The conflict situation may somehow have triggered it.

With regard to Sex Work, the large presence of the Army compounds the problem. The armed personnel come looking for women and the market for sex work is growing. When the demand is there, the supply is also there.

The conflict also results in broken homes and several single mothers without much economic support. Children in such homes also have to grow up without much support. So an impact is definitely there.

As an organization working on HIV/AIDS, have you ever faced any obstacles from the Church (in the sense that condom usage is encouraged by organizations apart from abstinence, whereas the Church puts emphasis only on abstinence as a means to tackle with AIDS)?

Yes, there are a lot of problems between NGOs and the Church condemning pre-marital and extra-marital sex. Churches are also realizing that not every one can abstain and that by encouraging the use of condoms, the NGOs are not increasing the incidence of promiscuity. But we still have a long way to go. We have to educate them on this issue to help them understand that we are not promoting promiscuity.

Also people who take decisions in the Church are of the older generation, so the younger generation does not meet eye to eye with the former. As a result a huge gap remains with the youth. Changes are happening fast and the economic conditions we are situated in as well as the luxuries we are running after are at extreme ends. If some compromise comes about, it will be better.

Whether the groups ever issued a diktat on the dress code of women?

I don't exactly remember who it was...it could be NSCN or NSF...but something like this had emerged.

Does the organization ever have to tailor its programmes keeping in mind the restrictions (such as mobility of women etc.)?

There has been no apparent opposition or obstacles faced by the organization. It is there subtly. If we call a meeting (both males and females), it is the men who speak the most of the time. Women also don't speak too often and do not take the initiative.

Once on World AIDS Day, I was asked to speak on HIV/AIDS. I spoke on how women and girls are the most vulnerable victims. After the talk was over, a male journalist came up and said that the talk was more on "feminist issues". When the report finally appeared in the paper, my name was not even mentioned!

Has the organization faced any problems from the insurgents?

We have not faced any problem with them. This is because,

they also have rehabilitation centres run by them catering to their cadres addicted to drugs. They send people to our organization to be trained. So we can actually share a bond with them on the drug issue.

How do you envisage the future for women?

Issue of much concern is domestic violence. It is prevalent but women seldom come out to report cases. Awareness needs to be brought about on the issue…even on the Bill on Domestic Violence that has been passed in the Parliament. Most women are not even aware of their rights. The violence will continue until women are made aware of their rights and sensitized on the issue. Awareness and Sensitization are most significant. Only then can change come.

2.3 Transcript of Interview with Pastor Dirang Lungalang (Interview on 1 February, 207)

Name	: Dirang Lungalang
Age	: 48 years.
Sex	: Male
Marital Status	: Married.
Level of Education	: Graduate
Profession	: Pastor
Name of Organization	: Christ Community Church.
Designation	: Overseer, Christ Community Church
Year of establishment	: 2003

- "Nagas have been created like all other people. God in His divine plan, put us here for his purposes".
- Acts 17:26 … & hath determined (God) the times before appointed, and the bounds of their habitation.

- Nagaland Baptist Church Council (ref. The Sentinel, 29th Jan, 07): Appealed to them not to use the phrase "Nagaland for Christ" till all inter factional violence stops, because they should not use the Lord's name in vain.
- Now the Church is actually taking up issues with the groups in conflict, more than before. The Church can emerge as a *Change Agent.*
- Diktat issued by a faction about two years back but there was a huge opposition. The civil society actively participated in condemning such an act.
- Rampant corruption in the system. Political powers that be take this to their advantage. Nagas are proud of their heritage and Christianity has fuelled this to some extent.
- In the earlier times, the Naga polity was a democracy. Only Konyaks had the chiefs (Angs), other clans had their Gaonburahs (village heads). Villages comprised of different clans. Each clan sent their best representative to the Legislative Assembly. After Nagaland was declared a State, all other forms of polity that existed previously were done away with. Today, if one has money and muscle power, one can contest and win elections. The Gaonburah has been reduced to a nominal head.
- The IM and K factions of NSCN have their parallel courts. People actually appeal to them with their petitions and problems.
- Knowledge can lay a lot of fears. As a landlocked state, we have to depend on India. We have to have an honorable existence/ good neighbourly relation with one another.
- Economy is important. We have to focus on the economy. We must encourage companies to invest here.
- The impact the conflict has had on women:

"The impact has been very depressing. Life has become very uncertain and that has become an impetus, driving people to go the Church. They now feel that only God could help them. As a pastor, I have noticed that women have become more prayerful than the men".

- As a Church, we are only 4 years old now. Our church is youth oriented and we cater mostly to youths. We try to approach them holistically—to help them realize their spiritual heritage. We are contemplating the opening of a vocational training institute. Once people have a sense of standing on their feet, they can decide and choose what they want to do in life. Whatever profit they earn, 10% would have to be given to the Church.

- How do you envisage the future?

It would be a great state. The process has begun. People are being exposed to good things. Once they realize their potential, they can strive ahead. The Church has a significant role to play. Nagaland will be sending the message of love to the people.

Map-3
Naganland District Map

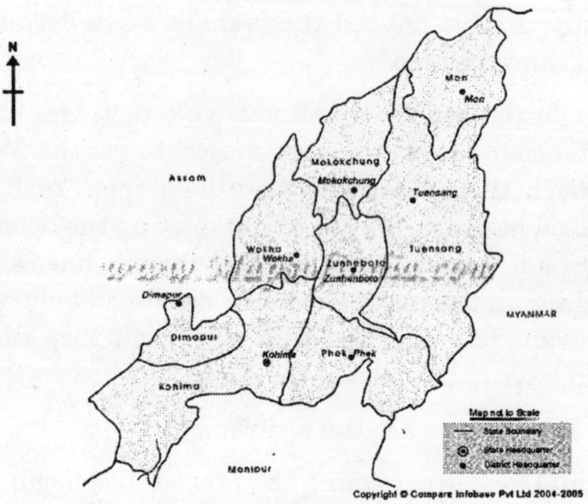

Map-4
Geographical Map of Egypt

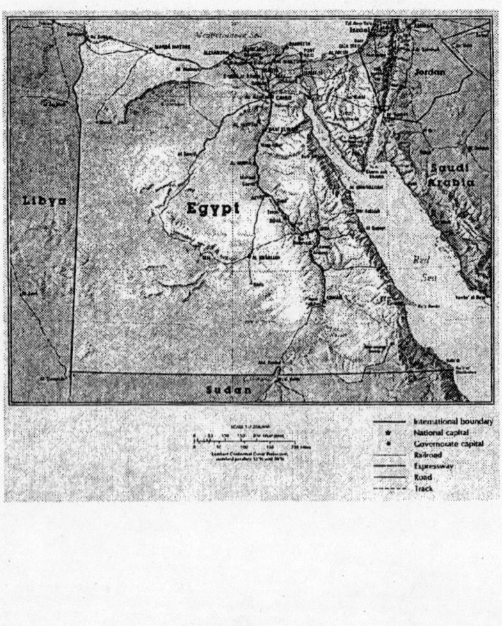

INDEX

■■■